Pyramid Mountain

The Virginia Mountains of Nevada

PYRAMID MOUNTAIN

"A Modern Cowboy Western Mystery"

by

Ian Feldman

SSI Publishing, LLC

P.O. Box 815

Holly Springs, GA 30142

USA

Table of Contents

EPIGRAPH

PROLOGUE

PART ONE: The Present - August

Chapter 1: BOBO'S BAR — RENO

Chapter 2: THE NIGHT VISIT

Chapter 3: ROSCO MONTANA'S OFFICE

Chapter 4: HOLLYWOOD DUDE RANCH

Chapter 5: THE PYRAMID CASINO

Chapter 6: THE SAN FRAN CONNECTION

Chapter 7: FRANKLIN'S LAW OFFICE

Chapter 8: ED HANSON

Chapter 9: THE EVICTION WARRANT

Chapter 10: ASHLEY AND COCHISE

Chapter 11: HOPPY'S CLAIM

Chapter 12: COLLECTING THE CHIT

Chapter 13: THE PLACER CLAIM

PART TWO: The Pyramid War

Chapter 14: THE SANDS MOROCCO INCIDENT

Chapter 15: THE PROPOSAL

Chapter 16: THE DEAL KILLERS

Chapter 17: ASHLEY'S BIG SURPRISE

Chapter 18: THE SICILIAN REVENGE

Chapter 19: THE FINAL GUNFIGHT

Chapter 20: SUNSET ON PYRAMID MOUNTAIN

EPIGRAPH

PYRAMID LAKE GOLD

VIRGINIA MOUNTAINS, NEVADA

"Chinese immigrants escaping from railroad gangs into the Pyramid Lake region of Nevada during the late 1850's formed camps of miners who were known to go into abandoned gold mines and scour out any left-over gold. Over the years, one of those camps were able to accumulate enough gold to create several large wooden trunks worth of gold nuggets.

Unfortunately, for the Chinese Miners, Paiute Indian Warriors often patrolled around Pyramid Lake; and one day when the Chinese miners were making a new camp along the lakeshore the Warriors entered the camp and robbed the miners of all their possessions, then massacred them. But at that time in history, the gold nuggets they had were worthless to the Indians. Hence, the Paiutes abandoned the heavy trunks of gold, placing them in a cliff cave at the lake.

So to this day, stories of lost gold finds, trunks of gold nuggets, gold coins and hidden veins of gold, persist in the areas around Truckee, Reno and Nixon, Nevada and throughout the Virginia Mountains."

PROLOGUE

In the beginning, 'The Hollywood' was a prosperous Dude Ranch built in the 1930's era of Nevada's once-thriving divorce trade.

Filled with a set of western styled rustic brown hued lodgings, beautiful ranch meadows filled with horses and longhorn cattle, along with barns placed along Pyramid Lake, it's clientele, back then, was mostly wealthy women from New York City and the North-Eastern States, with a few Los Angeles starlets thrown in to spice the place up.

Since divorce was still considered 'Taboo' in most of the States within America, as well as most of Europe from the early Twentieth-Century, Nevada's Laws 'that did not require proof of adultery, spousal abuse or mutual consent', became the new haven for these ladies.

For three decades, legally married women from other states with 'Restrictive' or 'No-Divorce' Laws, would secretly check-in to 'The Hollywood DR' for initially up to

'Six-Months', then later on, by the 1950's for 'Only Six-Weeks'. Then afterwards, they'd check-out one spouse lighter.

It was within this romantic Mountain Lake environment, that one rich NYC Socialite named Cynthia 'Masterson' Rothschild decided to get rid of her playboy husband and stay for the long term within the confines of 'The Hollywood DR' for love and personal protection.

The longer Cynthia stayed, the more she fell in love with the place and in one particular 'Cowboy' named Jake Montana.

Before long, Cynthia decided to buy 'The Hollywood DR' and make Jake, the Ranch 'Foreman'. Although they never married, she did become pregnant with Jake's son 'Rosco' who would also much later in life, become a local Reno entrepreneur, but also a broke gambler.

For almost ten years, they stayed at the Ranch together, then one day Cynthia's mother requested her to come back to New York City and attend her dying father's funeral. Mrs. Masterson sent her a Train ticket from Reno to Denver, then on to NYC.

Fearing that she'd never return, Jake pleaded with her to 'deed' him the Ranch, until she returned. She agreed, but mysteriously, she never returned.

What happened, in fact, was her husband actually found her, once she had returned to New York City; and had her murdered in order to inherit her money. Using a New York based Attorney, he set out to prove she was never legally divorced from him; then he erased all knowledge of her secret escapade into Nevada, as well as all traces of the divorce settlement documents.

Once Jake heard of her death, he was heart-broken, but set out to make the Ranch a success, even without Cynthia.

Unfortunately, he was not well educated and slowly over time the Ranch lost patrons and eventually broke down into disrepair as the losses mounted. When Jake died, he Legally WILLED 'The Hollywood DR' to his son Rosco, who was slowly getting himself deep into debt, with gambling losses in Reno.

And so, over time, this became the beginning history of the story of 'Pyramid Mountain'.

PART ONE

The Present - August

Chapter 1

BOBO'S BAR - RENO

AERIAL SHOT - ABOVE NEVADA: We begin
with the stark magnificence of the
VIRGINIA MOUNTAINS in Northwestern
Nevada.

High above it, we fly into the snow
covered alpine valleys, then down into
desert lower valleys over scrub trees
and sage.

Below us, the rugged sharp edges of
PYRAMID LAKE transformed by thousands
of years of weathering, slides away.

We enter a long box canyon near the
Lake's Western midpoint.

An upland pasture, holding a herd of
Painted Horses and Cattle grazing.
Hidden in that valley lies the entrance
to the ancient 1930's HOLLYWOOD DUDE
RANCH.

Eastward, we re-enter the narrow canyon
back to the Lake, then fly low over the
wind driven mountain whitecaps to the
South.

Below, the Truckee River, narrowed to a
rugged rivulet enters its low point, at
Pyramid Lake.

To get upstream, we travel forty miles
southward through desert outcrops to
where the river rises two-thousand feet
to meet its source, at Lake Tahoe Dam.

At last, and at the Half-way point
between Pyramid Lake and Lake Tahoe,
the Truckee River passes around and
under the city asphalt roads of RENO,
NEVADA.

On the outskirts of RENO, snow is
starting to come down hard. Only a few
people are on the streets.

It's getting late in the afternoon as
an old homeless Panhandler crouched in
an alley across from BOBO's Bar, waits
in the shadows.

He's pulling up his rotted coat collar
to stay warm and keep the wind out, as
he eyes the bar entrance for suckers,
then comments out-loud to himself. . .

"Jesus, it's fuckin' snowin' in August."

INSIDE BOBO's BAR:

ALAN WAGNER, a seasoned mature ranch boss, sits at the bar with MEL JACKSON, a low level ranch hand from that nearby 'Dude Ranch' called *Hollywood*.

Alan is smoking a cheap cigar and stares at the formidable inventory of booze lined up on the back bar in front of him.

He watches the reflections angled in the mirror above the back bar, staring at the inside entrance door, waiting as MEL comments. . .

"They said it's gonna snow thirty inches, before this mess is over. Maybe freeze solid, below twenty tonight. . ."

Alan doesn't react, as he watches a young woman with beautifully chiseled features, glide though the inside entrance door. Without slowing, she walks to the rear, pulls off a heavy long coat revealing a gorgeous body under her blouse. She holds ALAN's attention.

Her thin body and long slim legs seem poured into her tight jeans.

Passing the rear bar, she removes a cowboy hat uncovering a thick coif of beautiful long brunette hair, glancing at Alan.

Entering the kitchen door, she turns flickering a smile, back at him, as MEL continues his one sided conversation. . .

"That's fuckin' freezing, Al. We need to get back and put up the heard before nightfall or we're gonna be fucked by tomorrow."

Alan focuses on the SWINGING kitchen door, then turns back and speaks to Mel with a blank look on his face. . .

"You know, Rosco's closing 'Hollywood' for the season, after this one. . . What that really means, is he's out of payin' cash and there's no booked reservations beyond this week. . .

We've gotta get south to Vegas, Mel. This bullshit's gitt'n too deep, to live in, up here!"

"Yeah, Al, the guy owes too many G's to Goldfeller's Pawn."

Alan focuses on the mirror again. . .

"What I'm thinkin' is, maybe he should thin that heard and sell it out, Mel."

Mel freezes a stare at Alan, as his Boss continues. . .

"We could buy it, lean out the 'Paints
and the Mustangs', sell off the Mules
and all those petting Goats and such,
'n keep the Quarter Horses. . ."

Mel coughs out loud, then sips on his
BOURBON whiskey looking, as Alan adds.

"Then lease out the lake land to those
San Francisco developers 'n turn the
rest of the Five-Hundred acres into a
seriously professional ranch. . .

We could run it together, Mel. Get some
Beverly Hills Movie Dudes up here to
use us, to train their Stuntmen."

Suddenly, Mel opens up. . .

"What's Rosco gonna say to an offer on
something he just about doesn't own
anymore. Besides, the Movie business
don't care about 'Real Westerns' no
more. . . Here in Nevada, you'd be
better off turnin' the whole damn thing
into a 'Brothel Ranch' with a bunch of
HOT whores . . . than a Dude Ranch. . .

Nobody gives a fuck about Dude Ranches
anymore in Nevada, now that Divorces
are easy anywhere! It's all about
caterin' to the children these days.
That's why it's fall'n off so bad. . .
Rosco never figure'd that out,

neither . . . he's old school."

Alan looks back toward the kitchen
door, as the young brunette re-enters
and goes to the bar to get some towels.

She stops to look in the back bar
mirror, flips her hair seductively,
then ties it, as she again glances
toward Alan.

"Yeah . . . I get your fuckin' drift,
Mel."

As she re-enters the kitchen . . . Alan
stays focused on the spot where she
glanced at him.

"How old would you say she is?"

Mel reacts with a with wide grin on his
face.

"You know where this is goin', you' old
rascal. . . She's obviously too young
for you, Ole Boy."

"Maybe? I just like Bar girls!"

A look of surprise fills Mel's face, as
if Alan should've known; he knows
everything else.

"Alan. . . Her Momma owns this place
since the Grandad, the old Gizzer BoBo,
died back in June. She's divorced and
came out here from someplace in upper
Wyoming. . . took over with her kids.

Besides, that girl only works in the
kitchen. . .She don't serve or run the
Bar."

Suddenly we hear LAUGHTER from outside
and then FOCUS on the front entrance.
Alan sees a GROUP OF MEN reflected in
the mirror. They push into the inside
entrance from the street, BRUSHING off
snow.

Some remove their coats as they move to
a big booth across the room from the
bar. 'Mob' types.

They continue LAUGHING as Alan watches
them in the back bar mirror . . . then
turns and looks over at . . .

MIKE "THE KNIFE" GOLDFELLER, 'Chicago
Mob' - thick black coiffured hair
style, heavy set eyes, six feet,
overweight. His Tony Lama black gold
tooled 'Bling' Boots and gold Medallion
bootlace tie, set him apart from the
other types.

The others seat themselves around the
table and follow Mike's lead, as he
finishes up some joke. . .

". . . So the Cowhand says to me, what
has two legs and bleeds . . . so, I
says, half-a-horse."

The LAUGHING starts up again, but more
mercy reactions out of respect for Mr.
Goldfeller, than enjoyment of the joke.

Mike spies one of his 'Wise Guys'
looking behind him and turns, as he
sees . . .

Alan and Mel sitting at the bar.

Mel's sipping a Bourbon the Bartender just brought him and Alan's nursing a Beer, while eyeballing 'Goldfeller' himself, in the mirror.

Mel realizes the LAUGHING has stopped, as he looks over to the booth, Mike is looking straight at him.

"Mr. Goldfeller. . . How y'wall doing over there?"

Mike focuses on Alan as he reacts . . .

"We're okay. You'se, Guys?"

Mel quickly adds. . .

"Jus' fine, Mike. Jusss' fine."

But clearly, Goldfeller's booming voice is fixated on Alan not Mel, as he waits for acknowledgement.

Never turning, Alan stays focused, eyeballing only the mirror image.

So, Mel tries to fill the silence repeating his comment.

"Hey Mike, heard it's gonna snow over three feet before it's over out there . . . 'n a solid freeze by midnight."

Mike Goldfeller ignores Mel, as he calls out. . .

"Alan Wagner . . . being the
'*Hollywood*' Straw Boss 'n all that."

Mike grins mockingly towards Alan
Wagner.

"You oughta know when Rosco's gonna get
me my payoff . . .'n da juice.

Tell that asshole, I can't wait 'til
hell freezes over . . . And the 'Juice'
is doubled now!"

More mercy LAUGHS fill the booth, as
Mike's crowd acts out.

After a moment of silence, Alan finally
reacts by turning towards Mike.

"It's FOREMAN . . . Mike. . .

And I'm no ones' messenger! Tell him
yourself.

Besides, I don't discuss Mr. ROSCO
MONTANA's private business matters,
while yelling across a Bar."

Alan turns back to facing the bar
mirror watching Goldfeller SNAP HIS
FINGERS and point to one of his Wise
Guys.

He directs him, pointing to the kitchen
doorway.

A strong arm 'Chicago Mob' Type gets up
from the booth and heads through the
door to the kitchen area.

In moments, an attractive 'Forty-Something' blond, ANNE SCOTT emerges in front of the 'Mob Goon'. He has her by her left elbow, as she breaks free and walks up to Goldfeller. She's obviously pissed.

"Mr. Goldfeller, you can't just waltz in here 'n expect me to kiss your ass. . .

You better think again! You're out of control, Mister . . . Just because you once lent money to my Father. . .

He's dead now and I paid off his debts with hard earned cash. . . Well before, we re-opened BOBO's."

Alan watches her, as she stands her ground.

Mike Goldfeller looks past her at the 'Mob Goon'. He then stretches his neck around her and looks even further back.

The beautiful younger Gal, Alan was captivated with, now stands in the kitchen doorway, hands on her hips, looking ready to pounce.

"Mrs. Scott . . . I noticed your pretty daughter back there . . ."

Mike squints a sarcastic scowl at Anne.

"You oughta know, not to cause a scene in front of your children.

By the way, how many children 'DO' you have Mrs. Scott?"

"That's none of your business . . . Pack up your things and get out of here before I call the Police on you and your assholes."

"I heard you have three children, Mrs. Scott. 'ASHLEY' there, Billy and Joyleen.

I should also make you aware that Mr. Jordon, the Chief of Police of Reno is a very dear friend of mine and I've shown him Mr. BoBo's Lien Documents.

And he agrees you still owe me the balance of that $100,000 loan, Plus, Interest.

So unless you start paying interest or pay off 'da loan, we're foreclosing this Bar in two weeks."

Mike Goldfeller gets up and motions to his Goons. They all file out the front door, 'Mob Style', as Mike turns back to address Mrs. Scott's astonished expression.

"Good Evening, Mrs. Scott. . . And do keep a watchful eye on those beautiful children of yours."

Alan continues to watch everything take place in the mirror's reflection.

He then turns to Mel, who's putting on his overcoat and arranging his Western Stetson in the bar mirror.

"Jesus, Alan. Don't get fucked up in these people's mess, too. . . I can feel it burning in you. It's in the way you looked at that poor Mrs. Scott.

Alan turns to him and CRUSHES what's left of his cigar. He then motions to the Bartender to close out their checks.

"Sometimes, someone's got to clear up this kind of shit, Mel. . . That son-of-a-bitch can't keep fuckin up people's lives, unbridled.

Mike Goldfeller needs a Wolf's claws on his back. . . and being from Wyoming myself, I'm just that kind of 'Horror' . . . to fuck him up good."

Alan and Mel exit the Bar together.

Chapter 2:

THE NIGHT VISIT

OUTSIDE BOBO'S BAR: It's stopped
snowing.

A large Six-wheel pick-up truck GRINDS
to a halt, BRAKES SCREECHING, as the
driver parks it directly on the street
in front of the Bar.

It's dreary and except for the neon
lights of the Bar and one street light,
the area is dark. Snow is still on the
street and sidewalks as the old
Panhandler shuffles up in black cloth
wrapped sandals.

Alan Wagner exits, looking at the old
Guy, as he pulls out some change from
his pocket.

He notices a Ten-Dollar bill in the
mix, looks it over and hesitates. Then
for some reason, decides to give the
old Guy all of it.

"Bless you, my Good Man! Bless you."

Alan turns into the bar entrance, then
disappears inside.

ASHLEY SCOTT and her mother Anne are finishing the clean-up on the already clean "spic and span" kitchen.

A KNOCK on the Bar side of the door catches them by surprise, as Alan Wagner enters.

Ashley acknowledges him first, as she nods, removing her apron then sitting on a bar stool used for cutting work. . . Anne stays standing.

"Hey, I'm Alan Wagner."

Ashley is smiling at Alan. . .

"Well, Hi again. I'm Ashley. And this is my Mom . . . Anne."

Alan seems perplexed. . .

"What happened back there?"

Anne is clearly exhausted, as she openly reveals her concern. . .

"Ash said the SOB, did the same thing to you."

"Well, not exactly. . . It was my Boss he was coming after, but he wanted to use me, to up the 'ante', so to say. . .

He's just a lot of SMOKE and HORSE GAS without those Goons of his. I don't even know how he got started in this town. He seems like a leftover, from the 'Old Mob Era' Twenty years ago."

Ashley moves over to her Mom's side, as Anne begins TALKING.

"ANDY BOBO was actually my step-father.

When he died, he left us this Bar and a 'WILL' that even my local Attorney said was free and clear.

So I took all of our savings and fixed the place up, 'Kitchen 'n all', to make it pass city codes.

I'm divorced, so all we had was my money and some monthly child-support savings."

Alan watches her, as he's obviously drawn into her story. . .

"My Ex left the country for Bolivia last year and hasn't paid a 'Red' Cent since then. And unfortunately, both BILLY and JOYLEEN are still in their early teens, in school. . . Ash here is almost twenty-two. But she's my rock and together with BUD, our Bartender, we make this thing work."

Alan turns to Ashley grinning, then looks her up and down. . . as Anne remarks . . .

"Oh. . . And I'm sure you noticed, Ash sometimes distracts a lot of Guys with her looks.

Anyhow, this thing came out of left field with Goldfeller. . .

The Attorney's working on it, but for now we're up to our ass in debt, if it can't be cleaned up."

Alan focuses back on Anne's face. . .

"I've got some ideas on how to deal with him, Anne. . . but for now I just wanted to know how, I could help."

"Once my Attorney looks over those 'Lien Documents', we'll be able to put a plan together, but for now we just want to stay out of his way."

"I agree."

At once, Ashley jumps in . . .

"Speaking of help . . .Is there any jobs you have taking care of the horses out there on your 'Dude Ranch', Alan? I used to ride in competition when we lived in Wyoming. . . I have several trophies from 'The National Paint Horse' Organization out of Kansas."

Alan is clearly enthralled, as he remarks!

"Well that is quite impressive, Ash!"

"When we left Wyoming, I had to sell both my horses. I miss them a lot, but if you've got any horses that need care, I would love to hang out on the Ranch with them and help out. . . especially 'Paints'."

"Ah yes, the Paints. Well. . . we're soon to be down to two, but we'll still have Quarter Horses that need care and feeding. . .

So, yes, we could use you, Ashley. I'll make some arrangements for tomorrow, if you'd like to come up. . ."

Ashley is visibly excited, smiling. . .

"I'd love too. . . but for now, I'll need a ride."

"I've got that covered, Ashley. I'll need to meet you early though. . .

Say Seven AM?"

"That sounds great. . . I'd rather do it early, since Mom needs me here after Four."

"Well, that's our plan then!

I've got a long night ahead with this weather, but we're going to take on these DASTARDS. . .

'n we'll beat 'em."

Alan makes his way to the Bar's inside front door, with Ashley trailing, as he realizes Bud's already locked up.

"I'll see you early, Ashley. And take care, Mrs. Scott."

Ashley unlocks the door, then turns to give Alan an unexpected hug.

She seems to hold him a bit longer and tighter than he expected. A LOT longer.

As she releases him, she looks directly into his eyes. . .

"This really means a lot to me Alan. All I have now is my Mom . . . And, as you heard, my Dad's no count. . .I just want you to know Mom 'n I, won't forget this kindness.

You can be sure, of that."

"Listen Kiddo. . .

You should know, I'm from Wyoming too! And, I won't ever let this Guy screw with you and your Mother again. . .

Night, Ashley."

"Good Night, Alan."

Chapter 3:

ROSCO MONTANA'S OFFICE

INSIDE MIKE GOLDFELLER'S LIMO — NEXT DAY: A Chicago 'Mob Type' driving with another beefy MUSCLE MAN sitting beside him. It's overcast and still dark.

Snow's piled up along the roadway edge as they drive into a cleared parking lot of a small rundown strip-mall in front of Rosco Montana's Office on the outskirts of RENO.

Goldfeller watches the doorway of the office for movement. The blinds are down. Light can be seen from inside.

Goldfeller rubs his hands together to stay warm . . . Puts on his black leather gloves.

"You sure his secretary said he was in today?"

The 'Mob Type' Driver answers him tuff . . .

"Yeah Boss, that's what she said . . .

Told her, she'd better mark us on his calendar!"

Goldfeller, very agitated. . .

"I told that Son-of-a-Bitch he needed
to pay some juice . . . by last week.

But Nuthin'. . ."

VITO, the Chicago 'Mob Type' Driver
runs around to open Goldfeller's door
as the Muscle Man, stays in lead to the
doorway.

Then, like an obedient dog, Muscle Man
pauses at the door for the BOSS's
order.

"Jus' open the fucker."

Muscle Man pushes open the door.
Goldfeller and Vito enter.

Inside, they see Montana behind a large
western style 'Gold Rush' desk. A
single desk lamp is dimly lighting the
room, but Montana's hidden in the
shadows.

Goldfeller belts out loudly. . .

"Hey, Asshole. Get out your cash. . .

No checkbooks this time. You've piss'd
me off with that trick one time too
many . . .

Wasting my valuable time's gonna cost
you DOUBLE on the juice . . .Get It!"

Rosco Montana's chair is angled to the wall. Only his Western Stetson can be seen from the chair-back, as Vito walks over. . .

"Hey Boss, he's either sleeping or planning somethin'."

"Then wake him up, Chicago Style!"

The Muscle Man goes to the chair, spins it and without waiting, NAILS Montana in the nose with a massive right.

But there's no need to throw another. Montana's hand flops off his chest, as he falls forward, blood on his face.

It's now gushing from his nose, ruining his western shirt.

Goldfeller shouts at him. . .

"That fuck you up enough, Man . . ."

Goldfeller smiles satisfied, then motions to Vito.

"Get him up . . ."

The Muscle Man starts to lift him, as Vito cuts him off.

"Boss. . . He's road kill!"

The Muscle Man finally speaks. . .

"Hey, he sleeps with da' finches, Right Boss!"

"It's FISHES, YOU, idiot!

He sleeps with the FISHES!"

Mike's yelling - then looks at Montana.

"DAMN DEAD BASTARD!

Now . . . How do I get my money?"

Chapter 4

HOLLYWOOD DUDE RANCH

OUTSIDE THE DUDE RANCH STABLES: It has finally stopped snowing. An early morning sunrise is peaking over the Pyramid ridges as temperatures move back up to the thirties. Clouds are covering the distant mountains.

The new snow cover adds to the stillness and silence, except for an occasional HORSE WHINNY AND BLOW from within the stable.

Alan's truck is parked nearby.

A lone ranch hand can be seen doing snow removal at the HOLLYWOOD's Main House, a quarter mile down a nearby snow trenched road.

INSIDE THE STABLES: We see about twenty stalls, half filled with horses.

The place is empty except for Ashley and Alan, going over equipment inventory and viewing horse stock one by one.

"So that's about it, Ashley.

You know the drill on mucking these
stalls and the location of the feed and
equipment. . .

Come on up to the House when you're
through. I'll fill you in on the rest
of the Ranch and introduce you around."

"Easy enough, Alan. . . I'll see you in
a little while."

Ashley quickly turns back to Alan. . .

"Oh, by the way I do Short Order
cooking for Mom over at BOBO's, if you
need a cook from time to time?"

"Now, that sounds great. . .Ash! We
don't have a cook. Rosco fired him last
week. Some of the boys fill in for
breakfast, but none of them are worth a
damn."

A Horse in a stall near Alan SNORTS,
then another WHINNIES.

"We could really use your help. . . And
there's a fully stocked Kitchen, back
at the Main House."

"I'll get up there by eleven and check
things out, then. And is there an
intercom here, to the Main House?"

Alan stops at the entrance . . .

"Oh yeah. It's next to that toilet door
at the end of the stalls. . .

No lock though . . . So be ready to shout out, if you hear someone com'in."

"That's funny, but I'm used to worse

. . . Outhouses without doors."

"Well . . . Okay on that, Ash. I'll be at the Main House, if you need me.

Payroll's today. . .

See you later then, Kiddo."

Ashley waves to Alan, as he moves off toward his truck.

She turns, pulls her hair back, then puts on a pair of high rubber boots, as she heads for a nearby mucking shovel.

INTERIOR OF THE MAIN HOUSE-OFFICE: We view a converted bedroom Alan uses as his office. He sits at his desk reviewing work entries in the payroll-ledger book. . .

Out-front, a young RANCH HAND is TALKING to someone, as Alan picks up on the conversation through a partially open window.

"You musta had a hell-of-a-ride up here in that big car, Mister?"

Suddenly the voice of Mike Goldfeller begins bellowing back to the Boy. . .

"Yeah kid, that wasn't the half of it. We almost lost it all, on that last hair-pin curve."

"Yes, Sir, that's a real doozy, even for our ranch trucks with chains on 'em. Maybe y'all need to park that LIMO and have Alan take you back down."

"Speaking of the Devil . . . Where is that son-of-a-gun?"

Abruptly, everything goes silent. No answer to the Man's question.

Inside, Alan immediately looks up from the payroll-ledger, then LISTENS intently to the nothingness.

Silently, He opens his desk drawer and pulls out a loaded Colt .45 Revolver. He aims the gun at his closed office door . . .

In the hallway, Mike Goldfeller leads the way to Alan's back-office, as his two Goons trail him to the door.

Smoothly, Goldfeller exchanges positions with Vito. Then steps to the back side of his Muscle Man, as Vito draws his .38 S&W pushing the door wide open.

But Vito's face is completely shocked
to see Alan's big Colt aimed directly
at him. . .

Vito starts to FIRE, but Alan already
has the drop on him, as he FIRES A
SINGLE SHOT - taking out his firing
arm. . .

Quickly, Alan FIRES A SECOND SHOT at
the Muscle Man - taking off his left
ear.

Now, with even Goldfeller dazed, Alan
calmly gets to his feet and takes
center aim at Mike himself.

Everyone is SCREAMING. Then all stop
dead in their tracks. Vito grabs his
arm and moves back against the wall, as
the Muscle Man falls to the floor,
holding his ear, CRYING like a baby.

Alan looks directly at Goldfeller. . .

"Where do you find these Fuckin'
Assholes, Mike? You oughta know better
than this. Picking a WESTERN GUNFIGHT
up in this neck of the woods.

We shoot Pennies outta Gopher's asses
at One-Hundred yards for target
practice, up here!"

Suddenly the SCREAMING stops.

Mike CATCHES his breath. Wild eyed he
begins excitedly TALKING, as he raises
his hands in resignation.

"Whatta you wanna do Alan? Go to war!

We just came up here to bring you the NEWS."

Alan has a satisfied smirk on, as. . .

"I'm no 'DUMB ASS'! You don't sneak up on me with your guns drawn, justta talk shop, Mike. . .

What kinda, NEWS?"

"Rosco's Dead, Alan? He musta had a heart attack. We just came from his office in RENO.

He was cold as a block of ice, when we found him."

Now, Alan really looks pissed. . .

"Once again Goldfeller, I'm no 'FOOL'!

What did you do? Scare the shit out of him with your threats!"

"We just made an appointment with his Secretary . . .

And when we got there, he was sittin' in that big office chair of his. . . DEAD!"

Still pissed, Alan stuffs his Colt in his belt and scans the room . . .

"Well, if that's the facts . . .I'm goin to need some time to sort this out . . . talk with the police an all.

So, you're not gettin' nothin' outta
here, today."

Alan finally moves around his desk,
pulls the Colt back out and motions,
with the .45 in hand, for all of them
to get up and move out, down the hall
to the front.

"Best, y'all jus' get back down the
Mountain, Mike. . . we'll sort this out
next week.

If what you say is true. . . then, for
sure, after Rosco's properly buried,
we'll talk.

So, for NOW. . . GET OUT!

And leave that S&W .38, right where it
is."

Scared and Angry, Mike Goldfeller and
his Goons get up and start backing out.

As they turn to move out the door and
into the hallway, they're looking down
the double barrels of two shotguns. One
held by Alan's Ranch Hand, BUDDY and
the other held quite adeptly in the
pretty hands of Ashley Scott.

Chapter 5

THE PYRAMID CASINO

INTERIOR CASINO BACK OFFICE — NIGHT:
Mike Goldfeller sits in an opulent
Casino Managers Office. He's nervous,
he's stressed out and he looks beaten,
as he waits for his Boss.

All at once, the double doors BANG
open, as an immaculately dressed
executive, TOMMY LAROCCA barges in with
two Bodyguards dressed like members of
the President's Secret Service Team in
tow.

LAROCCA comments facetiously. . .

"So whatta you want me to do about this
mess, Mike?

Do you even know who's on first? You
gotta Lien on this Guy MONTANA's place
for over Five-Hundred G's . . .

You're short, ALL his last Six-Months
VIG. Then, he goes out with a heart
attack on YA! The way I see this. . .
IS, you're the ONE that's screwed. . .

On top of all that, you go up to his
Dude Ranch and start a fuckin' war with
his Foreman. . .

By the WAY. . . Do you EVEN KNOW who HE is?

He's JACK "LUCKY" WAGNER's brother, the 'BIG GUY' down in Vegas at the SANDS MOROCCO.

You fuck with him and he'll bring the New Jersey Mob in here.

They'll cause a major problem all over this town . . . We ain't got the assets to fight that shit, Mike.

You need to back OFF, NOW . . . And get your priorities in order.

Mike reacts, almost moaning for sympathy.

"But, HOW, do I make up that much lost CASH, Tommy?"

"You'll find a way . . . look over my 'Marker BOOK' for starters . . . See who's late.

But as long as 'LUCKY' WAGNER's tied in, Nothin' happens to that Foreman.

Capisce!!"

Mike's face is filled with total resignation as Tommy adds. . .

"My advice. . . Find a way to work with him! You're a creative Guy, Mike! Now get outta here and make us some money.

The 'easy way', Bloodless!"

Mike Goldfeller, CLEARS HIS THROAT.
Takes a last look around at everyone,
gets up and heads for the door; then
'like a ghost' he exits silently into
the Hallway.

Chapter 6

THE SAN FRAN CONNECTION

THAT SAME NIGHT - INSIDE THE MAIN HOUSE AT HOLLYWOOD DR: In his office, Alan is urgently going through a file box of letters and other correspondence that belonged to Rosco Montana.

He LIGHTS up his cigar, as he spies the letter he's looking for.

CLOSE-UP: The letter is from a Real Estate firm in San Francisco that expressed an interest in the massive range of Pyramid Lake Property, contained in the Hollywood Ranch Deed.

Alan picks up his phone and dials their number. . .

SAN FRAN RE FIRM OFFICE: After several rings, a strong voice answers . . .

"This is ED HANSON with Hanson & Anderson Properties. . .

How can I help you?"

MAIN HOUSE AT HOLLYWOOD DR: Alan immediately reacts. . .

"Yes, Ed . . . this is Alan Wagner up in RENO. I realize it's late, but we have to talk."

Alan is apprehensive as he begins. . .

"You'd expressed an interest some months ago on our Property, bordering around Pyramid Lake, and I wanted to follow-up on it."

SAN FRAN RE FIRM OFFICE: Hanson seems okay with the late hour. . . even friendly.

"Sure, Alan. I remember you and Mr. Montana. We would be very interested in that property."

MAIN HOUSE AT HOLLYWOOD DR: Finally, comfortable, Alan jumps in with details. . .

"Well, unfortunately Mr. Montana died recently and I'm now handling his affairs.

SAN FRAN RE FIRM OFFICE: Ed's empathetic.

"Sorry to hear about his passing."

MAIN HOUSE AT HOLLYWOOD DR: Alan quickly adds specifics. . .

"As the Ranch Foreman, I've taken over and we're downsizing. Could you meet me up here tomorrow to discuss the original proposal?"

SAN FRAN RE FIRM OFFICE: Ed's cautious.

"Well . . . I can't see a problem with that. You're about Three-Plus-Hour's drive time, from my place. . . I'll just have to move a few things around on my schedule. . .

How's just after noon sound to you?"

MAIN HOUSE AT HOLLYWOOD DR: Alan anticipates with apprehension. . .

"That actually sounds, Great, Ed! I'll meet you here at the Main House.

We'll have a nice lunch ready for you too. We've just hired a new cook!"

SAN FRAN RE FIRM OFFICE: Ed seems finally relaxed. . .

"Sounds terrific. . . I'll See you there, Mr. Wagner."

MAIN HOUSE AT HOLLYWOOD DR: Alan hangs up and continues searching Rosco's files.

THE NEXT MORNING - OUTSIDE THE HOLLYWOOD STABLES: We view a wide vista of the open range beyond the Stables and into the North Pastures. Misty mountain fog covers the nearby Virginia Mountains and Lake Pyramid.

Ashley Scott and Alan Wagner are riding the two remaining 'Splashed White Overo Painted Horses' left, on the 'Hollywood Ranch'.

Ashley's obviously a very solid, but elegant stylized rider, while Alan has a hard cowboy style to his ride. He's used to working the cattle and longhorn herds in open range and ranch work.

They are making their way back to the stables, as Alan opens up . . .

"Damn Ashley, you're one HELL of a solid rider. . . Even down those gulches back there. I'm really impressed with you!"

"When you love this breed as much as I do, Alan, you become one with your horse. . .

No terrain is out of balance for me, as long as my mount can traverse it. . . This, to me is the most natural form of transportation in the world."

Ashley slows her steed, then looks over to Alan. . .

"I need these horses as much as they need me."

They both halt, at the edge of the open field, facing the stables in the far distance.

Alan grins at her, as he eyes the 'broad' open-quarter-mile trail, back to the stables. Ashley's horse, SNORTS his power into the face of Alan's ride, as he feels her challenge.

"Do you wanna make a run, for 'who mucks their stalls'?

"I don't know, Alan?

With COCHISE here, I don't think you'd have much of a chance. . .

Besides, when was the last time you mucked a stall?"

Alan LAUGHS. . . as he noses his white faced 'Overo' up to her 'Blue-Eyed-Beauty'.

"I say we give it a go. . .On THREE, Ash!

One. . .Two. . .Three!"

Both riders and horses EXPLODE AT FULL GALLOP as they run hard and fast across the open field, then down onto the main dirt road.

Ashley clearly got the JUMP on him, but Alan pulls up close. All at once, Cochise seems to gain INTENSITY in his stride, as Ashley gets up close to his right ear and SAYS SOMETHING.

It's over in only a few seconds, as Ashley passes the Riding Arena in a flash, reaching the Stables first.

Whipped, Alan pulls up, flabbergasted.

"Damn it, Kid. . . Wha'd you say to that damn Horse. . . He was on FIRE!

We'll have to change his name, to COMET."

Ashley starts laughing and beaming at Al!

"I just told him we'd better beat your sorry ass . . . Or he wasn't gonna get MY sugar today. . ."

They both start LAUGHING TOGETHER, dismount and begin removing the saddles 'n blankets, wiping down their respective Horses.

Alan then shouts out to his Ranch Hand, Buddy, as they walk their horses to the pasture gate removing the bridle gear.

Alan releases his horse first.

"Hey Buddy. . . How 'bout mucking the stables for me! I've got a big guest coming here about noon and we need Ashley up in the kitchen today, to prepare us a spread!"

Buddy gives him a thumb's up . . .

"No problem, AL. I'll be down there in ten minutes . . .

Ashley turns to Alan, smirking . . .

"Why Alan Wagner. . . You never said I was in the kitchen today. This race was rigged!

You still owe me a 'real mucking'. . . You can't fall back on Buddy's kind heart jus 'cause you're the Boss."

"Well, you're right, Ashley. . . But I had some things in mind besides having you prepare a Special Lunch for our 'Guest' and us. . .

I actually wanted you to give him a demonstration of your riding 'n equestrian skills too . . .

Plus, there's something else, I have planned for you in the future.

A kind 'da Short Competition Show, right here in our Riding Arena."

Suddenly caught in amazement, Ash is now smiling big at him, again. . .

"Wow, you're just full of surprises, today."

And, what exactly, do you want on the *Lunch Menu* for this 'Special Guest'?"

"I'll leave that for you to decide, Ash. But he's from San Francisco, so I'd say he's a Mexican-Styled Salad-Type for starters. . .

You take it from there."

"Well, let me get cleaned up, Alan. And I'll get on it."

"Just use the Guest Bedroom up at the Main House, Ash. . . And there's some Women's Riding Competition outfits, we used a few years back, in the closet up there, too.

So feel free to make up your own Combination Outfit with what fits you and your style."

"No kidding . . . Women's Competition Clothing? I'll do it. Sounds like fun.

See ya at the House, Alan!"

They both head off in opposite directions. Ashley waves, then walks back to the Main 'Hollywood' House.

Chapter 7

FRANKLIN'S LAW OFFICE

EXTERIOR OF AN ATTORNEY'S OFFICE –
AFTERNOON: Another cheap strip mall on
the outskirts of RENO. Bright sunlight.

Mike Goldfeller's Limo drives into the
parking lot.

As they arrive, a cute twenty something
secretary heads off to lunch, out the
front door of the Attorney's Office.

Unseen in the Limo, Mike Goldfeller's
on the phone SHOUTING. . .

"So, what you're tellin' me IS, you
can't seem to find Bobo's Lien
documents OR the details on MY 'bona
fide chit'. . .

Well, listen to me asshole!

That chit you owe 'THE PYRAMID' for
those Sports Bets, is mine now. And
we're out here in the parking lot,
waitin' for ya!

So bottom line, I'm here to collect,
plus the juice for two months . . .
That's $38,500 'hard ones'.

INSIDE THE ATTORNEY'S OFFICE: Nevada
Attorney, HOWARD 'HOWIE' FRANKLIN
rushes around in his private office
frantically collecting documents.

He YELLS, INDISTINCTLY into his
intercom.

At that moment, the FRONT BELL RINGS.
The door SLAMS open. Blinds SHAKE
LOUDLY against the wall of the front
office, while Howie's Secretary's phone
RINGS OFF THE HOOK. . .

FRANKLIN tries to reach her, as her
intercom BUZZER SCREAMS. Entering the
Chaos, Mike Goldfeller and his Mob
Type, Vito. While, His Muscle Man is
outside in the Limo, engine RUNNING.

Without waiting, Vito takes two steps
across the room and pushes open the
inside office door with his LEFT hand.

Realizing, Vito's RIGHT ARM is still
immobile in a black sling around his
neck, Mike Goldfeller decides to help,
pushing it forward and walking in
behind him.

Mike eyeballs Howie Franklin.

Howie GASPS. . . As Mike Goldfeller's
VOICE, shatters his nerves . . .

"Here's the way it's gonna be, ASSHOLE.
. .

You either pay up my chit today, VIG n'
all OR you get that bitch OUTTA my BAR
by this weekend. . . You understand!"

"Wait a minute, Mike. . . The owner,
Mrs. Scott, has no agreement with you.
She's spent thousands fixing that place
up.

It's hers by 'Certified Nevada Will &
Testament Law'."

Bullshit, Howie! Now, YOU have really
piss'd me off. . . Bobo's been up to
his eyeballs in debt, owing me since
two years back!

Death don't discharge Debts, YOU
idiot!"

Goldfeller SNAPS HIS FINGERS and Vito
hands Mike a 'Deed Document'.

"Bobo assigned this Deed to me. Here's
the proof . . .

Goldfeller holds out the 'Deed' for
Howie to see. Howie starts to reach for
it . . .

"Don't touch it . . . Shithead!

You need to get that bitch and her crew
outta there by this weekend. . . 'Else,
you got bigger problems than practicing
Law."

Howie's shaking as he takes a close
look at the deed document held in
Mike's hand . . .

CLOSE-UP: Andy Bobo's 'Assignment Signature', then the 'Nevada Notary Seal' and 'Various Signatures'.

"Okay, okay Mike. . . This looks official.

I hafta admit it, Mrs. Scott hasn't been able to find the 'Deed' Bobo left her, yet.

Maybe, this IS it?"

Goldfeller chuckles out loud. . .

HAH. . . Ya Damn right, it's IT!"

"Okay, Mike! Let me go down to the Courthouse and see if it matches the filed 'Deed', the Notary put in."

"Listen, ASSHOLE. Filed or Not . . . Wait! You've piss'd me off again!

This IS the 'Deed' for Bobo's Bar and from here on out you've got TWENTY-FOUR HOURS to confirm your Courthouse Shit.

Then get them outta there . . . Oh, and then, pay up YOUR debt and all that juice! That's $38,500 you OWE me! You Got That?

DO YOU Understand ME?"

Howie nods his head reluctantly, still shaking, as he scribbles down the Deed number . . .

"You're Right, Mike! I'm on it . . . I got it!

Just give me some time to get this all done and get some money out of my own savings."

Again, Goldfeller shouts. . .

"Twenty-Four hours, ASSHOLE! That's It!

You got Twenty-Four hours!"

Mike Goldfeller and Vito both glare at Howie menacingly one last time, then turn and STOMP OUT the same way they came in.

Chapter 8

ED HANSON

INTERIOR DUDE RANCH DINING ROOM: Ed Hanson and Alan are sitting around the dining table eating lunch.

CLOSE-UP: A detailed survey map of the Hollywood Dude Ranch Property with topography and five separate forty acre plots is spread out on the open end of the dining table.

Ed looks over the five separate Pyramid Lake Plots carefully. Alan is finishing eating his Mexican salad, as Ed points to something on the survey.

"This is one hell-of-a spread here, Alan. How many acres total?"

"The Ranch has Fourteen-Hundred acres .
. .

And the contiguous rights to Government BLM land is Thirteen-Thousand acres for grazing and cattle, if we wanted to go back that way. But we're downsizing."

"So how do you reach this land along the lake, Alan? This map doesn't clear that up exactly . . ."

"Well, that's the hitch now, Ed.

Once you buy in, we need, together of course, to petition both the County and the State to give us a separate access to Highway 445 - 'Pyramid Lake Road' - for all your properties."

At that moment, Ashley enters from the kitchen with coffee.

"Got some HOT cherry pie and whipped cream for Dessert, you Boys . . .How 'bout some?"

Both Alan and Ed look up at her, as Alan winks and adds his own special smile . . .

"Bring it on, Honey, 'cause, we've got to "Test Out" ALL your lovely delicacies, before you can officially become the Head Ranch Chef."

Alan CHUCKLES, while watching Ashley. She frowns at him.

"By the way, Ashley, this HAS been an outstanding lunch. . . And my Vote's cast! You already ARE, the Head Chef on this Ranch, without lifting another finger!"

Ashley smiles at Ed, bending just enough to pour his coffee, as her sleeveless western style blouse, held by only a rawhide neck strap, exposes her beautiful deep cleavage.

She holds that pose, as. . .

"Hey Ed, I overheard you mention to Alan about your wife leaving the 'Ford Modeling Agency' in San Francisco?"

"Actually, Ashley, she didn't leave, they just closed their agency in San Fran. The local 'GAZE' Model Agency is the leader there now. . . Too much competition, I guess."

"So, she's OUT of the business?"

"Well. . . For, NOW. In fact, she's helping me. . . at least until she gets her 'Freelance Modeling Team' back together.

"I'd love to talk to her."

Ed takes her in, close-up, as she stands up over him with her big sexy smile.

"You know. . . You should, Ashley. Western Style Models are an area unrepresented in the industry . . .

And with your height and stature. . .

Plus, from what Alan tells me of your riding skills, you'd be a real winner for the Western Outfitters Market out here.

I'll talk to her when I get back and give you a call."

"Tha'd be real awesome, Ed! Oh, and call me, Ash, please. . . Hey, let me get those pies, 'fore they cool off, Boys.

Ashley disappears into the kitchen, as Ed grins over at Alan. . .

"She's a Real 'Innocent' Beauty, Alan. Don't know how you'd keep from tapping that one?"

"Tempting my friend, but she's too young for my blood!"

Ed slyly winks at Alan. . .

"Ooohhh. Gotcha Old Man."

They both start LAUGHING.

"Well, then. . . I can't wait to see her ride, Alan!"

Just then, Ashley re-enters from the kitchen with the Pies, a can of whipped cream, and HOT coffee pot in hand, as Alan jumps up to help.

"Here, Lemme' help you, Kiddo! We've got to get down to those Lake Plots soon, for it gets too late."

Alan takes the coffee pot, as he looks seriously at Ashley. . .

"And you've got to intercom, Buddy, to get 'Cochise' ready for your SHOW."

LATER - OUTSIDE AT THE PYRAMID LAKE
FRONT: Alan's holding the Survey Map,
showing the additional PYRAMID LAKE
plots, on his truck hood.

Ed is looking across to the Eastern
side of the lake, then turns to look
West, up the dirt road they came down.

He stares at the massive cloud covered
Virginia Mountains looming behind the
HOLLYWOOD Dude Ranch.

"The views are simply breath taking,
Alan. These five plots would be perfect
for four unit condos! I could see us
developing these. SOLD, in under three
months, if the winter weather stays on
hold."

Alan looks concerned as he answers. . .

"Well, Ed . . .

The County, the State and the BLM will
hav'ta approve multiple owner dwellings
on a single forty acre track out here.

So, that could be another hurdle we'll
need to work on . . . Together of
course."

"I see . . . well, you've got your work
cut out Alan, but if you can get us set
up, show me an 'Original Deed' - not a
photocopy like that one up at the
house. . . My investors are in the
ballpark for all five plots at easily
over a million. . .

And make sure you've confirmed the road rights. . .Before we meet next week."

"Sounds like I've some serious work ahead!

For Now, let's go up an' watch that girl work her Paint.

OUTSIDE AT THE RIDING ARENA: Alan and Ed are sitting on the outside fence of the Riding Arena, as Buddy walks up to Ashley with Cochise.

She's decked out in a beautiful black leather Mexican riding outfit with knee length Western Boots and a Black Stetson.

Ed just gawks, at Ashley, as even Alan is surprised by her choice. She raises a hand to Alan, signaling she's ready.

All eyes stay on Ashley, as Alan explains to his 'Guest', what is happening. . .

"What you're watching is an exact demonstration of a 'Sanctioned Barrel Racing Event'. . .

These Events call for 'precise distances' between every barrel point, on that Cloverleaf Pattern out there, Ed."

In the blinking of an eye, Ashley grabs the saddle horn, putting her leg up and into the stirrup, then swings her other leg over pulling herself onto the saddle.

"Our Arena Course here, is exactly Four-Hundred and Twenty feet in length - start to finish."

"Damn, that girl looks beautiful out there, Alan. . . An' that horse is enormous. . . He's incredibly built!"

Cochise tosses his head and looks back at her, as she puts her arms around his neck and moves up to his right ear, quietly WHISPERING to him in their special language.

"Well, you're right Ed. Cochise IS quiet tall at Sixteen-Hands . . . That's Five-Feet-Three-Inches. . . So he could possibly make this run in record time.

After several silent moments, Ashley takes the reins and begins moving him slowly around the arena.

Cochise BAYS, as they pass Buddy, signaling he's ready.

"And what's that record, Alan?"

"I'd say a 'World Record Time' on this size course, would be around Fourteen-Seconds or a fraction less for the entire run. . .

And I've never seen a more confident
equestrian than Ashley, So, watch out.

They could break it right here, in
front of us!

Ashley's leisurely movement quickly
turns into a gentle ride, then
transforms into a TROT . . . then she
begins a LOPE . . . then a CANTER. . .

Cochise is building energy at each
TURN. Alan quickly gets his timing
watch ready.

"Here's what's goin to happen, Ed. It's
gonna happen fast, so watch close . . .

Ashley's approach to the first barrel
is critical. She must bring Cochise's
sprint up to speed at the right moment
to enter the correct path on that
'Cloverleaf'. . .

Then, she must make perfect TURNS
around each BARREL."

Instantly, Ashley and Cochise enter a
HIGH SPEED GALLOP together, heading up
to the starting point.

Horse and rider become merged in a
beautiful blur, as they break through
the timing line.

Alan immediately, hits his START WATCH.

DUST BURSTS OUT everywhere, as they
race first to the Right Barrel of the
Cloverleaf Pattern.

God! This is incredible . . .It's so
exciting to watch HER and that HORSE,
Alan!"

That girl's like an ANGEL out there
Flying by on PEGASUS . . .

Ashley and Cochise set up to take the
TURNS like two ballerinas merged in a
perfect pirouette.

"Notice as she takes that TURN, she
must be in position . . . as well as,
DEEP in her saddle, her hand on the
horn and the other one guiding Cochise
through and around that BARREL TURN."

IN SLOW MOTION: Ashley and Cochise take
the Second TURN, from the opposite
direction.

Duplicating the same procedure as the
first TURN, Ashley and Cochise REVERSE
their limbs and muscles, in perfect
harmony.

"Ed, notice her legs. . .how close
they're against Cochise. . . She's
tight on his girth. . . She's
supporting his rib cage.

It's a 'Special Technique' to set a
focal point for each TURN."

AGAIN IN SLOW MOTION - THEN IN REAL
TIME: Ashley and Cochise SPRINT to the
backside of the arena to the THIRD and
FINAL BARREL.

"Believe it or not, the athleticism
required for this maneuver is
incredible for both Rider and Horse.

When she finished that second barrel,
she looked through the turn, then
focused on the spot to enter that final
barrel at the rear of the arena."

At last, Ashley and Cochise EXPLODE, as
they run for home.

"She looks to the finish line. . . And
makes her mad dash Home."

Ashley GALLOPS across the timer line in
a blur of motion and SOUNDS, just as
Alan clicks his WATCH, stopping it.

"God, that was so exciting, Alan!

BRAVO, Ash! BRAVO!"

Ashley and Cochise slow up to a HALT,
beside Buddy. Right off, Buddy starts
toweling down Cochise. Ashley's on an
'Incredible High' smiling at Alan.

Alan's waving and SHOUTING WILDLY along
with Ed Hanson, who's arms are
outstretched to embrace either Ashley
or Cochise or BOTH.

No one knows exactly who he's gonna hug
first. Both men race down into the
arena to congratulate them as Alan
shouts out to her!

"Incredible run, Ashley! Incredible!
Thirteen-Point-Nine Seconds! That's a
World Record, Kiddo!"

Ashley and Cochise Barrel Racing

Chapter 9

THE EVICTION WARRANT

EXTERIOR BOBO'S BAR: It's late afternoon as heavy clouds darken the RENO skies. Only a few people are drifting by, as a County Sheriff's Car U-TURNS, SQUEALING.

It quickly SWERVES UP TO THE CURB, BREAKING DEAD in front of BOBO's Bar.

A second car, a black sedan PULLS IN from the opposite direction, as a dark suited attorney steps onto the sidewalk.

Two Sheriff's Deputies exit their car, papers in hand, and move into the entrance.

Across the street, the old homeless Panhandler watches them.

INSIDE BOBO'S BAR: Sitting at the bar is Mel Jackson. It's his day off and he's downing his first Bourbon Whiskey of the afternoon.

Mel and the Bartender, Bud, finish up their CONVERSATION.

Mel, without turning, focuses through the mirror on two Deputies coming through the inside doorway.

"Hey Bud, hand me that house phone over there."

"No Problem, Mel. . ."

Bud drags the phone and cord from the end of the bar, to Mel. Nervously, Bud starts wiping down the bar, as Mel ROTARY DIALS the Main House number at the Ranch to get Alan.

"Think I should get the Boss, Mel?"

"That's wha'd I'd do, pretty quick!"

INTERIOR HOLLYWOOD DUDE RANCH OFFICE: Alan catches the call, just as he's walking into his office. . .

"This is Alan Wagner."

INSIDE BOBO'S BAR: Too late. The two Sheriff's Deputies are in front of Bud, before he can move into the Kitchen.

"Hold One . . . Alan. It's me Mel!"

The Dark Suit comes up behind them, glancing over at Mel, who's now TALKING INDISTINCTLY on the phone.

The 1st DEPUTY SHERIFF speaks first to Bud.

"Excuse me, Sir, but we need to talk. . ."

The Deputy pauses, to check the papers he's holding.

"We need to talk to Mrs. Anne Scott."

"Give me a moment, Sir . . ."

Bud then rushes into the Kitchen, as the Dark Suit watches Mel speaking on the house phone. . .

"Yeah, I'm off today, Alan . . . that's why I'm down here. . . Hey look, they seem to have a Warrant of some type. . . Yeah, you coming down here with the girl?"

Just then, Anne comes out of the Kitchen with Bud in tow. Her face is in shock, as she walks up to the Deputy.

"What's this all about Deputies?"

The 1ST DEPUTY SHERIFF reacts, serious.

"Are you Mrs. Anne Scott, ma'am?"

"I am. So what's going on here?"

"This is a Final Eviction and Lock-Out Warrant ma'am. You are illegally on property that does not belong to you."

The Deputy then hands her the OFFICIAL PAPERS and continues. . .

"You have Twenty-Four hours to remove all of your personal property from these private premises or we will be forced to have a supervised service do it for you, at your expense.

INSIDE RANCH HOUSE - BACK-OFFICE: Alan Wagner has just pressed the Ranch intercom button for the Stables. He still has his telephone in his left hand, as we HEAR Buddy on the Intercom.

"Hey Alan, you want me to send Ash up to the Main House?"

"Yeah Buddy, get her up here, PRONTO!"

Alan returns to TALKING on the telephone.

"So what the Hell happened, Mel?"

INSIDE BOBO'S BAR: Mel is trying to size up the situation. . .

"I think you gotta talk to Mrs. Scott, to get her side, Alan.

Gim'me a minute, she's right here with BUD."

INSIDE RANCH HOUSE - BACK-OFFICE: Alan hears some MUMBLING and SHUFFLING in the background, as Anne finally gets on the phone.

"That Bastard got to my Attorney! Jus' talked to him. He says Goldfeller has the official Deed on this place . . ."

At that moment, Ashley Scott slides into Alan's office as he covers the phone pointing to a chair in front of his desk.

Alan holds a finger up to his lips, then. . .

"It's your Mom . . . We've got a problem."

Alan uncovers the telephone mouthpiece.

INSIDE BOBO'S BAR: Anne SPEAKS stressed. . .

"He verified it at the Washoe County Courthouse. . .

They gave me a 'Warrant of Final Eviction' and Lock-Out. The County Sheriff and Goldfeller's 'Mob Goon Lawyer' jus' delivered it. . . Warned us to be completely OUT 'n 24 hours or they'd remove us!"

Anne sounds beaten. . .

"God. . . Now, what'll I do, Alan?"

INSIDE RANCH HOUSE - BACK-OFFICE: Alan speaks with confidence. . .

"Hold on Anne. Hold on. . .Give me some time to think this through.

If need be, we can send some Ranch hands down to re-locate your things to a storage room over at our office in Reno for a time.

But this requires a bigger plan, Anne. . . You know that."

INSIDE BOBO'S BAR: Suddenly Anne SCREAMS back at him in complete frustration. . .

"God Damn it, Alan! I've had ENOUGH!

My Attorney's taken every last cent I had, to fight this thing! Even asked for more money jus' now when he told me the latest on the Courthouse drama."

Anne's VOICE is strained. . .

"We're going back to Wyoming, Alan!

The money's gone, we're liv'in in a run-down trailer, the kids hate it here. . . that's IT!

We're gone, Alan, no more bullshit for me!"

INSIDE RANCH HOUSE - BACK-OFFICE: All at once, Ashley reacts in PAINFUL TEARS. She's heard it all, as she grabs the phone from Alan and SHOUTS in the mouthpiece. . . Speaking through her tears.

"I'm tired of moving Mom! I'm tired of this Gipsy life.

I love it here on the Ranch! This is
the life, I've always dream'd of. . .

INSIDE BOBO'S BAR: Anne quickly reacts
to Ashley's painful confusion. . .

"Honey! I didn't know you were there
listening to this. . . I wanted to talk
to you privately . . . Jus' you and me
Ash. We'll work it out for YOU, I
promise!

You're all I got left, in life!"

INSIDE RANCH HOUSE - BACK-OFFICE:
Ashley is almost violent as she yells
back. . .

"It's no use Mom! I know what you're up
against. . . I know you've had enough .
. . But so have I!"

Before Alan can react, Ashley SLAMS
DOWN the phone and runs out of his
office in TEARS.

INSIDE BOBO'S BAR: Anne is in SHOCK. .
. "Ash, Ashley . . . Please listen,
Honey!

Listen to me . . ."

INSIDE RANCH HOUSE - BACK-OFFICE:
Alan's is stunned at how quickly the
young girl evaporated, as he slowly
picks up the phone and SPEAKS to Anne.
He can hear her still TALKING
incessantly to Ashley's 'phantom
voice'.

"Anne, Anne. . . Hold on. . .It's Alan!

She's Gone. . . Give her some time,
Anne.

She's broke-up! She's fragile now. . .

You got to give that kid some time to
rationalize or she'll really break from
you.

She's like a wounded filly now. We'll
go get her in a little while and you
two can get all this worked out, I
promise."

Alan can HEAR Anne suffering and crying
on the other end of the line.

INSIDE BOBO'S BAR: Anne finally
realizes, there's nothing she can do.

"Okay Alan, Okay. . ."

OUTSIDE THE MAIN HOUSE — THE PORCH: We
have a long range view of the Stables,
the Open Riding Arena and beyond into
the Western Pasture.

A dark Misty-Mountain-Fog floats down from the Virginia Mountain peaks, with light snow falling within it.

Alan walks out on the Porch and watches a lone rider GALLOPING AWAY HARD toward the High Western Valley on a beautiful 'Splashed Overo Paint'.

It's Ashley and Cochise moving as one, off into an eerie sunset glow.

Alan turns away frustrated, then re-enters the Main House.

INSIDE THE MAIN HOUSE — OFFICE: Alan DIALS a Las Vegas number from his desk telephone.

INSIDE THE SANDS MOROCCO — EXECUTIVE OFFICES - LAS VEGAS, NV: An Executive Secretary softly answers the call in a serious business-like manner. . .

"JACK WAGNER'S office, this is VERONICA."

INSIDE THE MAIN HOUSE — OFFICE: Alan begins his thoughts, as he speaks. . .

"It's me Veronica, Alan. . .

Is big BRO, around?"

INSIDE THE SANDS MOROCCO — EXECUTIVE
OFFICES: Veronica's voice suddenly
transforms to, very sexy, as. . .

"Hi, Cutie! He's down on the floor . .
.

Working a couple of WHALES from Long
Island!

Want me to get him, for ya'h?

INSIDE THE MAIN HOUSE — OFFICE: Alan
loves her vocal transformation, as he
thinks through his next moves. . .

"No, No, don't do that, it'd piss 'em
off!

Jus' THIS, then, Sweetheart . . .

Jack knows what's goin' on . . . I just
need the name of that damn WASHOE
Courthouse 'Schlock' that owes the
MOROC Fifty G's!

Tell 'em, I'll get the VIG too. But, I
need his name by tomorrow."

INSIDE THE SANDS MOROCCO — EXECUTIVE
OFFICES: Veronica's voice is still
super sexy. . .

"You oughta know, Jack had that already
pack'd up for 'ya, Cutie. . . It's
Charles Ferguson . . .

He's at 102 Faulkner Lane in Reno. Want
his phone too?"

INSIDE THE MAIN HOUSE — OFFICE: Alan
continues thinking his next moves.

"Nah, I'm gonna visit this 'One'
Personally, Babe. . ."

INSIDE THE SANDS MOROCCO — EXECUTIVE
OFFICES: Veronica loves to juice up the
back-story on these problem 'children'.

"Well, I've seen his profile photo!
He's a Fat-Mac-Boy for sure. . .

Veronica smoothly adds a long pause,
then she starts to whine. . .

"When you gonna come down let me model
for you again, I've got a new Brazilian
bikini. . . it's reee'ally tiny, too!"

INSIDE THE MAIN HOUSE — OFFICE: Alan is
now in overload as . . .

"Soon Babe, Soon! And give BRO a big
thanks for me!"

INSIDE THE SANDS MOROCCO — EXECUTIVE
OFFICES: Veronica clearly loves to
swell her charm on Alan. . .

"I will, Cutie! Bye . . ."

Alan hangs up the telephone and makes some notes. Then takes a moment to consider the plight of these beautiful women he's now in league with. . . whether he likes it or not, Ashley and Anne are now under his personal protection.

Chapter 10

ASHLEY AND COCHISE

OUTSIDE ALONG THE HIGH MOUNTAIN
VALLEYS: Ashley and Cochise are at the
top of a ridge watching the reflected
sunset glow on the mountains east of
Pyramid Lake. She's got both arms
around his main, WHISPERING something
into his right ear. Mountain clouds
quietly slide in behind them.

The clouds begin to engulf them, while
slowly blotting out the view to the
valleys below. Snow is beginning to
fall heavier than before.

All sounds seem silenced by the
beautiful natural wonderland. The only
path back down is along a narrow ridge,
as the snow begins to quickly fill-in
Cochise's hoof prints.

Ashley carefully begins their steps
downward. Everything is perfectly
still, the silence is beautiful to her.
When without warning, that fateful
SOUND: Cochise's METAL HORSESHOES SKATE
ALONG A SHEER ICE EDGE.

The edge runs to a snow filled gulch
along their left side.

Cochise notices it at the same moment.
He SNORTS, then WHINNIES to her knowing
he can't control his rear hooves.

WE WATCH THEM BOTH IN SLOW MOTION -
THEN REAL TIME: Cochise begins
STAGGERING then STOMPING to find
traction.

Ice shards are BLASTED into snow clouds
on the ridge, as they suddenly slide
sideways HARD-DOWN along the gulch
wall.

Ashley's right leg is JAMMED between
the girth of Cochise's massive ribs and
the rock outcroppings along the gulch
wall.

They slip off balance into the dark fog
of a crevasse. Fearlessly, Ashley
reacts, controlling the chaos, as her
right foot abruptly gets DRAGGED out of
its stirrup.

She can't pull it up, so she tries to
move it backward away from Cochise's
body, without JERKING out of the
saddle.

AGAIN IN SLOW MOTION - THEN REAL TIME:
Cochise stays controlled, but tries
desperately to get back onto his feet.

Ashley finally tightens her grip on the
reins and wrenches her foot free,
COMMANDING Cochise to stay calm. Yet,
they continue sliding sideways down the
incline.

At the base of the gulch, they SLAM TO
A STOP. A creek bed.

A surreal silence enfolds them.

Only the TRICKLE SOUND of the tiny
stream melting, as it FLOWS OVER ROCKS
is HEARD.

Silent fog laden clouds and falling
snow form a protective blanket all
around them, hiding their injuries from
sight.

But the pain is there, as Cochise
SNORTS AND SHRIEKS once, to let her
know he's wounded and suffering. But
how bad?

Ashley's dazed, EMOTIONAL AND TEARING
UP, as she gently strokes Cochise,
while WHISPERING to him.

"Oh God, baby . . . What have I done to
you?

What has happened to us?"

As our point-of-view, begins to move
outward and away from the hapless horse
and rider, we can see something
beautiful . . . the obvious GLEAM of
something very valuable catches our
attention. It's a large bright golden
nugget, lying simply in the trickling
water stream, near Cochise's neck.

At Once, the horse finds his footing,
SNORTS and proudly lifts himself and
Ashley up.

He looks down and paws the creek-bed
near the GLEAMING OBJECT, as Ashley
carefully dismounts, continuing to talk
to him.

Then, she sees it, herself, as well.

"OH'MI'GOD, Baby!

Look what you've found for us. Maybe
we've got an Angel looking over us,
after all.

INSIDE THE RANCH HOUSE - THE MAIN
GATHERING ROOM - LATE NIGHT: In the
meantime, Alan and Buddy are sitting in
big western style leather chairs on
either side of the main fireplace
reading.

A ROARING FIRE is CRACKLING, as the
front door OPENS.

An exhausted and somewhat disheveled
Ashley, enters quietly. They try not to
spook her, acting out, that they're
seriously reading that shit.

She takes off her boots and long coat,
then walks up to Alan, kissing him on
the forehead as he comforts her. . .

"Have a good ride, Kiddo?"

Ashley silently slides her hand into her jeans pocket and retrieves the Six-Ounce gold nugget.

She drops it onto the paper outstretched across Alan's lap.

"Wha'd YOU think, Mister!

Alan reacts like a STRIKING RATTLER, grabbing the fat nugget before it drops down into his crotch. Then JUMPS UP in shock.

He stares at her, then the nugget.

"Where in the HELL did you get this?"

She's smiling from ear to ear at him, before speaking, as Buddy rushes over to find out what all the ruckus is about.

"Well, let me just start out by say'in, it was Cochise that actually found it.

He saved us both from a near fatal fall down an icy gulch up at Needle Rock. It was in a creek bed."

"Damn, that's on our property! That's Pyramid Mountain!"

Alan rubs it around in his hand and shows it to Buddy.

"Are YOU 'n HE alright . . . No cuts or breaks?"

"We both got some scraps, Alan. But, I just finished cleaning him up . . . An puttin' him up for the night.

But no serious cuts and NO breaks. Thanks, to our Guardian Angel, for sure!"

"Damn, if you didn't bless us with this, Sweetheart. You're, the Guardian Angel!

Here, have my seat . . . Buddy, get another chair over here!"

Alan turns and gives her a big hug.

Then sits her in his chair as Buddy drags his own over for Alan. He then pulls over a wooden high-back for himself.

While they all settle in, around the BIG WARM CRACKLING FIRE.

"Well then, Ash, let's get the details on all this . . . And see what we can do to get us, an Official Nevada Gold Claim filed.

I think you're 'bout to get us all outta hock, Sweetheart!"

Chapter 11

HOPPY'S CLAIM

OUTSIDE BOBO'S BAR - EARLY MORNING: No one is on the street.

Alan's truck is parked in front of the Bar, but the old homeless Panhandler's gone. The alley across the road is obviously vacant.

There's a little ground fog, but the air is still, as a tiny glimmer of sunrise begins showing up over the snowy mountain ranges.

INSIDE BOBO'S BAR: LAUGHTER is coming from the kitchen. . . We move though the entrance of the Bar passing reflections in the back bar mirrors, as we enter the kitchen.

Suddenly we find everyone (Alan, Ashley, Mel and Buddy) there, standing around a stainless food prep table in the middle of the room.

The Hollywood Ranch Survey MAP is spread on the table center, as Mel Jackson starts a question. . .

"Alan, what's this Twenty-Acre dashed square on the East side of the 'Hollywood' property?

It seems to be up on 'Pyramid Mountain'!

In fact, Needle Rock's right in the middle of it . . .

As Alan points it out to everyone. . .

CLOSE-UP: The survey MAP shows INITIALS inside a square.

"Not sure, Mel?"

Ashley takes an even closer look.

"And, there looks to be some initials over here too, Alan. . . 'AB & HJ'. . .

Suddenly, without warning, a SCRATCHY VOICE ERUPTS from the back of the kitchen.

VISUALLY WE SEE: Anne, she's SCRAPING a freshly cooked pan of eggs and bacon into a now empty plate for . . .

'HOPPY' Harry Jackson, the initials (HJ), the old besotted Panhandler from across the street; who everyday gets fed 'gratis', by Anne.

Hoppy coughs loudly, before he eats.

"That's ME 'n Andy. . . 'AB 'n HJ'! Andy BoBo 'n Harry Jackson, that's us.

Instantly, everyone is caught by
surprise. Looking over their shoulders
to Anne and 'Hoppy' near the rear exit
door at a small table and chair,
they're stunned, as the old man
finishes SUCKING UP his eggs and
GULPING DOWN his coffee.

Alan jumps in first. . .

"Damn, Hoppy . . . Haven't heard you
say som'thin', since BoBo died. Tell us
'bout this, then!"

Hoppy grins at all of them, almost
toothless, as he LAUGHS.

"All 'dat belongs to Anne now. . .far
as I'm concerned. . ."

Alan chokes his thoughts out. . .

"What'da HELL you mean, Hoppy?"

"Well back in the day, Boss. . . Andy
Bobo and I prospected da 'Pyramid' for
Gold and became good friends of old
man, 'Burnett'!"

Alan adds in background to everyone, as
the old man seems to hesitate, COUGHING
AGAIN.

"Old Man Burnett, was JOSH Burnett, his
initials are (JB). He's the one who
sold off The 'Hollywood' Dude Ranch
portion of this MAP, to Rosco's Mom,
Cynthia.

Burnett himself was actually, the original owner of all this land, from the 1920's."

Again, Hoppy gets going, as he CHORTLES LOUDLY, with all the attention. . .

"Yeah, that's right, Mr. Wagner. Josh even had land up to the top of them mountains.

He had so much land, the BLM bureau even took some back, when he died. But, Mr. Burnett gave me and 'Ole' BoBo the mineral rights to those twenty acres. . .but, we never found an ounce of Gold up there. . .

He'd told us those rights were good 'til we died, and I ain't dead yet, just 'poor'."

Alan finally gets it.

"You've got what's called 'A Life Estate', 'Hoppy'. . . Damn, Everyone!

Bobo and Hoppy had a Mineral RIGHTS, 'Life Estate' on that land. . .

We've got to get to the Courthouse with this fact, NOW!"

Confused, Mel cursorily questions something on the MAP. . .

"That's this dashed square, then, here on the MAP. . . Right, Al?"

At once, Ashley adds her thoughts. . .

"And there's also, these two sets of initials on other areas of the MAP . . . for 'BoBo' (AB) and 'Hoppy' (HJ).

So what's it all mean, Alan?"

"Means were all Fuck'd, if anything happens to 'Hoppy' here, 'cause 'Bobo' IS DEAD. . . Or, if ANY of this gets 'out of this room'!

In fact, Mike Goldfeller doesn't know about ANY of this 'SHIT' yet. . .

Hah! He's actually got a flaw'd 'Deed' – and he doesn't EVEN know it!"

Anne jumps in suddenly, realizing Alan's meaning.

"BUT. . . those Mob BASTARDS could STILL take everything we've got goin' for us here! So we MUST be careful, Ash!"

Alan reacts swiftly . . .

"That's WHY, we've got to get your CREW and your 'STUFF' outta here this morning, Anne!

Plus, Move YOU, your kids and that trailer of yours, up to the Ranch. . .

Including finding 'Hoppy' a bed, PROTECTED, down at our Stables. . ."

Alan turns to Buddy.

You'll be in charge of 'Hoppy', Buddy!
Put him in that empty Ranch Hand's
'Cubby' we were using for extra tack."

"Got it, Boss! Me 'n double-ought-buck,
we'll keep him safe!!

Alan turns to Mel, with more
directions. . .

"Mel, you're in charge of getting our
Hands down here, to move out Anne's
Trailer. . .

Hitch her to your big rig and pull it
behind the Main 'Hollywood' House, so
they've got electric and water access.
. . And keep it sort of hidden, back
there."

"Got your drift, Boss! Should we get
started now . . ."

You 'bet', go ahead. . . and I'll call
the rest of our Boys on down, by phone.
They can move Anne's bar 'STUFF' to our
storage room, behind Roscoe's strip
mall office."

Again, Anne jumps in . . .

"You want me to stay here, Alan."

"Yeah, you'd better. . . that way, when
Bud comes in to work, you both can show
our Boys just what to pack, and how to
pack it!

Ashley moves over to Alan, ready to
roll up her sleeves, as . . .

"And ME, Alan. . . What can I do?"

Alan smiles back at Ashley, as all the 'Cowboys and Bucks' take her in.

"You Sweetheart, are coming with me. . . To the Washoe County Courthouse, then, the Assay Office. . . and finally the Claims Office. . .

We're gonna get this 'Gold Claim' locked in, before those 'Bastards' know what's hit'em!"

"But, what about that original Deed, Alan? Don't you REALLY need that, too?"

"I've got a plan for that. . . That's why we're headed to see 'Someone' I know, before the Courthouse opens at 'Eight' this morning. . .

A 'Someone', that owes me a CHIT. . .

AND, You and I, Ashley, are collectin' that 'CHIT', today!"

Chapter 12

COLLECTING THE CHIT

OUTSIDE CHARLES FERGUSON'S HOUSE: Alan and Ashley arrive a little after seven in the Morning at 102 Faulkner Lane, in Alan's pick-up truck. They park across the street.

It's a tidy neighborhood of small, nineteen-fifties style homes. No one's about, not even kids. It's unnaturally quiet.

INSIDE ALAN'S TRUCK: Alan looks at Ferguson's car, still parked in the driveway. He scans the street, then looks at Ashley. She's gorgeous.

"Here's what I want you to do. . . As soon as I get out of the truck, go knock on his front door - when he gets there, tell him you're collecting for 'The National Paint Horse Organization' . . . 'n you'd like a donation of say, Twenty-BUCKS.

"What if he says, NO?"

To you, Ash! Get outta here! You can talk him in to it.

Jus' buy me some time, but come directly back to the truck regardless . . . Do NOT go into his House; and don't worry about what I'm doing. . .

Got it!"

"Okay, but . . ."

Before she can ask her question, Alan's out of the pick-up and around the backside of Ferguson's House.

Ashley checks herself in the rearview mirror, grabs her bag, flips her long brunette tresses to one side, then exits. In a kind of 'prancing swagger' in her tight jeans and cowgirl boots, she catwalks over to Ferguson's front door.

She hits the doorbell, flips her blouse open for a little extra cleavage, then poses effortlessly, as she whispers.

"It's Va-Va-Voom time, Baby!"

INSIDE FERGUSON'S KITCHEN: Alan picks the lock and slips quietly through the back into the empty Kitchen. Then sits at a stool overlooking the inside doorway.

He can HEAR THE INTERPLAY between Ashley's VOICE and Charles Ferguson's.

"Is this a Race Horse Organization? Are these racing horses. . . you know, like, the Santa Anita 'Race Track' Horses?

Ashley's RESPONSE IS MUFFLED as Ferguson replies. . .

"Okay, yeah! I get it now . . . Let me go get some cash, Doll. Just stay right there!"

Ferguson prances back to the Kitchen and sides open the lower freezer drawer of his brand new French-Door Refrigerator.

Eerily, he suddenly senses 'something', as he realizes, a Man's just sitting there looking at him. He nearly jumps out of his skin!

SHOUTING AND TWITCHING WILDLY, he's as nervous as a 'Stuck PIG'.

"Holy Jesus, Mother Mary of God, Christ

Almighty. . . Who the HELL are you?"

Alan can hear Ashley, almost 'HOWLING IN LAUGHTER'.

As her GIGGLES trail off, he's sure she's gone to the truck.

"Are you really THAT Catholic, Charles?"

So's 'THIS IS WHERE' you stash all that 'Gambling Money' of yours . . .

I guess that's a damn site 'safer' than
a Bank these days. . . with the IRS
'SHIT' on Gamblers."

Ferguson's face goes 'RED', as his
VOICE gets even higher pitched. . .

"WHO ARE YOU?"

Alan just grins at him, exposing his
holstered .45 Colt.

"Where you been lately, Charley?"

Ferguson's still shaking as he stands
up, closes the Freezer Drawer, then
drops both hands to his sides staring
at Alan.

"You know . . . Your good friend's at
the MOROC in Vegas miss you Charley. .
.

In fact, Mr. Wagner told me, just this
week, you've got Markers for over Fifty
'G's, that 're over ninety days past
due. . .

And NOT a phone call. . . NOT even a
'little juice' to smooth things over,
NOT even your 'FACE' at his Tables down
there. . .

What's up Charley?"

"Hey, Hey, listen to me, MISTER. . . I
Love those Guys at the MOROC. . .

I Love Jack, too . . .But things are
just real tight, right now."

Alan gets up. . . Ferguson FREEZES.

"I'm not gonna hurt you, Charley . . . Jus' move away from that Freezer Drawer, there."

Charley watches 'fearfully' with 'big cow eyeballs', as he awkwardly shuffles to the side like a 'hefty walrus'.

Flicking open the drawer, with a vicious frown on his face, Alan focuses on Charley, as he feels around in the drawer.

He pulls out an aluminum foil wrapped package. It's obviously been re-wrapped a dozen times, as Alan throws it on the counter.

"Open IT, Charley!"

Charley carefully opens the aluminum foil wrapped package. It's filled with strapped packs of $100's, $50's and $20's.

"Looks like you have a 'Mini ATM' here, Charley. . . Let's do this . . .

Hand me 'TWO' of those $100's packs."

Charley reluctantly pushes them over to Alan.

"That's I'd say . . . 'bout Twenty 'G's, RIGHT, Charley!

Tentatively, still RED faced. . .

"That's what they are, Twenty 'G's. . .

Ten-Thousand a piece."

"Okay, Charley. . .

Then, we have 'da VIG', Charley. . .
Here's how 'da VIG' works. . .

I'm coming over to the Courthouse, this
morning with my 'photocopied' Deed. . .
An' I'm gonna need, an 'Original Deed',
made up from that photocopy. . . Got
IT!

Real, Simple!

An' you're gonna do that for ME, when I
get there . . . NO QUESTIONS, Asked. .
. You understand!"

"Okay, Okay, I'll do it! But please, we
have to do all this before 9:00 AM . .
. or my employees will be arriving.

They can't see us together. . . or I'll
get screwed.

"Done, Charley!

Simple as that . . .

Your Marker's NOW, ONLY Thirty 'G's. .
.

So, that's all there is to IT.

Oh, and 'Come See Us' SOON, Charley."

Alan gets up and quickly walks to the front, vanishing into the morning light, as Ferguson collapses in a kitchen chair.

EXTERIOR WASHOE COUNTY COURTHOUSE - LATER THAT MORNING: Alan and Ashley seem tense, as they quickly leave Alan's truck at a parking garage and walk. It's almost 8:15 AM.

They reach Virginia Street, in front of the Courthouse, as people are SCURRYING LOUDLY up the Courthouse's Granite steps to work.

IMSIDE THE WASHOE COUNTY CLERKS OFFICE: Approaching a doorway into Charles Ferguson's Office, Alan motions Ashley to stay outside, as he enters.

Ashley sits at an Old Wooden Clerks Bench opposite the CLERKS OFFICE door and tucks herself into the end of it.

She then, closes her eyes, exhausted, for a momentary catnap.

In moments, a tall, thin, business suited young man, his face almost obscured by the massive stack of papers he's carrying, rushes by her.

At the same time, he tries to maneuver
his bulging 'Brief Case', in his left
hand, around Ashley's outstretched long
legs.

But it's too late, as the 'Brief Case'
catches on her SILVER BOOT TIP.

SLOW MOTION: Falling, everything
EXPLODES OUTWARD across the floor,
papers, his briefcase and him.

Instantly, Ashley opens her eyes to the
devastation she's caused and jumps up
to help, REACTING LOUDLY.

"OMIGOD! OMIGOD. . .

I'm sooo'oh sorry, Sir!"

The young man, KEITH LINGERFELT, is
scrambling on the floor grabbing his
papers, trying his best to re-organize
things.

Ashley quickly gets down on the floor,
as well, to help him. Fortunately, no
one else is in that area of the Clerk's
Hallway, as they both scramble around
grabbing things.

Trying to swiftly put 'Humpty, Back
Together Again'!

Out of the blue, with the stress of
everything in her LIFE, plus her
massive LACK of sleep, Ashley BURSTS
OUT LAUGHING DEMENTEDLY. . . as the
young man reacts. . .

"Christ! What's so funny, Lady?"

"It's just like Humpty Dumpty . . .
We're trying to put everything back
together again. . ."

She continues with crazy giggles. . .

"You know how it goes . . .

'Humpty Dumpty' sat on a wall,

'Humpty Dumpty' had a great fall, 'n
all the King's Horses 'n all the King's
Men . . ."

Finally seeing this absolutely
'Gorgeous Gal' on the floor with him;
He finishes it for her, as HE starts to
LAUGH DEMENTEDLY, too.

"Couldn't put Humpty together again!

I love it . . . That's just the way
this day's started out for me. . .

A TOTAL wreck!"

Back to frantically grabbing things,
Ashley accidentally grabs some papers,
right between his 'crotch'.

As she stops dead in her reach, without
removing her arm, she slowly looks up
into his 'very handsome, but astounded'
face.

"OMIGOD! OMIGOD. . . I'm sooo'oh SORRY,
AGAIN, uh!"

Looking down into her big sexy eyes,
Keith tries to change the subject, away
from her apparent miscue.

"It's Keith. Keith Lingerfelt.

Uh . . . Are you going to leave that
there?"

Realizing her predicament, Ashley jerks
her hands back, to her hips, and stands
up, towering over him in her high-
length, 'COWGIRL' boots.

Keith tracks her with his eyes, as she
rises up, looking like 'Wonder Woman',
then casually asks.

"What's yours?"

Her innocent smile, blows him away. . .

"Oh, my gosh. . .

We'll, Mr. Keith Lingerfelt. . .

I'm Ashley Scott . . . Obviously, at
your service!"

Instantly, they both start LAUGHING
again.

INSIDE CHARLES FERGUSON'S CLERK OF
COURT OFFICE: Alan is clearly agitated
from his wait. It's almost nine. The
office officially opens in ten minutes.

Ferguson is still in his back room working. Alan can see him. He's just finishing placing official WASHOE County Seals and a Notary stamp on the Deed.

At last, Ferguson moves back to where Alan is 'clipping his nails', just as one nail pops-up into Ferguson's oncoming face.

"So, this is how you, thank me . . ."

Sorry old Chum, that wasn't planned. . .

You got it done, then?"

Ferguson starts smiling proudly. . .

"Probably the best I've ever done!"

"Sooo'oh, Charley. . . You've done this before?"

"NO! Not that way . . . Just the standard document processing 'n all."

Alan stands up, facing him, GRINNING.

Seeing that look again, Ferguson shuts up, lowering his head.

He stuffs the Deed into a manila envelope, then extends the package reluctantly over to Alan.

"Okay, Ferguson . . .

We're done here. . . That's da VIG!"

Alan grabs it. Then, disappears out of Ferguson's Office.

WITHIN THE CLERKS OFFICE HALLWAY:
Sitting together on the ancient and well-worn 'Clerks Bench', Ashley and Keith are BANTERING back and forth, when Alan walks up surprising them.

It's His typical 'mysterious arrival', but this time he's perturbed. . .

Alan looks down at Ashley, who's now smiling at Keith. . .

"We need to get going, Kiddo!"

"Alan, please wait. . .

First . . . You've GOT to meet, Keith here."

Alan frowns. . .

"Hi, Keith!"

He snatches a look at Keith, then shrugs him off!

"Now let's go Kiddo, we've got a schedule to keep . . . And getting to the State Claims Office was NUMBER TWO on our list!"

Alan nervously looks around, for likely office workers watching them.

"Besides. . . Ferguson wants us outta here, Pronto!"

Ashley clearly sees his unsettled reaction, then pats Keith's shoulder, as she locks eyes with Alan.

"Keith is a Mine Engineer with 'The Big Montezuma Mine Group' out East of here, Alan. . . He can help us . . .

And he's also, on his way to the Claims Office. . .

Alan looks back at him, this time more seriously. Keith tentatively extends his hand out.

"Pleasure to meet you, Mr. Wagner. I'm the Chief Assay Engineer for 'The Ruby Lake Mine Division', maybe . . ."

Alan cuts him off, as two Clerk's Office Employees march around them, glancing back, then enter the Clerk's Office.

"Okay, Keith, HOLD that thought. . . That ACTUALLY, sounds good for us. . .

Let's meet-up at that 'Little Coffee Shop' near the Nevada Claims Office, on Court Street. . .

Say, Ten-Thirty!

Okay!"

Alan motions to Ashley. . .

She's up, giving a sexy wink to Keith.

"Sounds Good, Sir!

See you BOTH there. . ."

But Keith acts almost forlorn, as they walk away from him. . . then, catching Ashley's quick glance, back at him. . . WAVES AT HER!

"Bye Ashley!"

OUTSIDE BELOW THE COURTHOUSE STEPS: Alan and Ashley walk together, in purposeful forced silence, for ten minutes.

FINALLY, AFTER SEVERAL STREETS: They turn onto Court Street, then spy 'The Little Coffee House'. . .

"Sorry, I had to drag you outta there, so quickly, Ash, but I didn't want to complicate Ferguson's life any more."

Ashley aggressively interrupts him. . .

"No you aren't SORRY!

You want me all to yourself. . .

You're afraid that Guy likes me,

An' we're gonna get friendly. . .

Or som'thin . . ."

"That's not true, Ashley . . .

Well maybe, a little . . .

I do want YOU all to myself, for NOW.

But, I also know, as a young woman,

you've got needs too. . .

And if that Guy's, to your like'in. . .

Well, maybe you SHOULD get to know him
better."

"He IS, to my like'in. . ."

Ashley stops walking, with a hard stare
at Alan.

"And, I love you too Alan, but he just
might be able to help us. . . He's
smart and he's funny and he knows all
of the folks at the State Claims and
Assay Office . . .

Plus, he's work'd small gold mines by
himself, so he knows how to plot ours
and get it up 'n runnin'. . ."

Alan grins back at her. Then nudges her
gently to start walking again, as they
finally arrive at the Coffee House. . .

"Ashley, I'm NOT your Dad. . .

And I'm NOT your Boyfriend. . .

I'm just, a 'Very Close Friend' that
wants to PROTECT you, until all of this
is over.

Then, we'll see how everything goes."

Across the street, Keith Lingerfelt
pulls into a Government assigned
parking place.

He's driving a black sedan, with Nevada
Permanent Tags on the front 'n rear.

Jumping out, briefcase in hand, he
quickly bounds over, breathing heavy,
while smiling all the way at Ash.

"Okay! I've finally got all of my
assignments under control, at last."

He breathes deep, as he watches Alan
cautiously. . .

"Let's get some coffee and talk all
this through. . ."

OUTSIDE 'THE COURT STREET COFFEE
HOUSE': Keith holds the door.

Ashley, then Alan, enter ahead of him.

SOMETIME LATER, INSIDE 'THE COFFEE
HOUSE': Alan, Ashley and Keith have
been drinking coffee and TALKING since
Ten-Thirty AM.

Alan is stretched back, comfortable in
his chair watching.

Ashley and Keith CONTINUE BANTERING.

The survey plot is in Keith's hands.
Ashley stretches over him and points
in. It's the location that she and
'Cochise' went-down-in at the gulch.

"So what do you think about this
location, Keith?"

As he looks up, he's eyeballing right
between her breasts.

"God . . . You smell nice, Ashley."

Knowing where his eyes are, Ashley
again smiles, to redirect his
attention. . .

"It's Ash, Keith. . . Just call me
Ash!"

"Oh yeah . . . Got that, Ash."

Alan COUGHS and CLEARS his throat,
watching them, as he quips.

"So, what were you saying, Keith?"

"Oh. . . Well, let's consider options."

CLOSE-UP: They focus on the MAP,
exactly where Ashley's finger is
pointing.

"Part of this area is inside your
Ranch's private property line, so it
falls under 'The Private Mineral Rights
Rule', that's property that you're NOW
Deeded."

Keith then goes into detail, explaining to Ashley what BLM means. . .

"I'm sure Alan knows this, but for your benefit Ashley, you need to know what BLM means. It's 'Bureau of Land Management' Land. That's Land that belongs to the Federal Government and managed by our Nevada State Government for all citizens. Claims can be staked on this Land, but the process is rather complicated.

Just understand, Private Property land you own is easier to Claim Rights on, but BLM Land can be Claimed on as well, if it comes down to that."

Ashley listens intently, but now she has an informed question. . .

"So what about just filing a 'Lode Claim', Keith, and getting all of this under our control, right now!"

"First, Ash, most folks would overreact and file an immediate 'Lode Claim' outside your property line on that 'BLM Land'. . .

But that only covers a maximum length of Fifteen-Hundred feet by Six-Hundred feet on either side.

What we really don't know is, where the 'ore vein' actually exists. . . Do we?

So our best bet is to file a 'Placer Claim', along the border of your land.

That's of course 'BLM Land'. . . but that also covers 'Twenty Acres', not just a few Hundred feet."

Ashley sits back down and remarks, as Alan goes back into his 'silent relaxed mode'.

"Well that finally makes sense, Keith!"

"Once we're through with physically finding the true 'ore vein', Ash, then we can either add to your claim up to One-Hundred and Sixty Acres . . . Or get a 'Lode Claim' on anything in or nearby the 'BLM Land', that's holding ore."

"So, how much will that cost us, Keith?"

"We can get it all covered for under Three-Hundred dollars. . . Then get up there, to begin surface inspections, put out our markers, then assay the 'gold ore' and 'minerals' we find."

"And how long, for all that?"

"Well. . . Could take a day, maybe even a week or more, but we'll find it"

"Gawd! I had no idea it was gonna be this complicated, Keith . . . What do you think, Alan?"

Alan grins at them both, as Ashley turns to him searching his eyes for HIS 'hidden opinion'. . .

But knowing, he knows something more than he's admitting, openly at least. . .as he speaks.

"Okay, Kids, ENOUGH . . .

We're burning daylight, here!

It's time to pay off those damn 'BLM-Feds' and 'The State Claims' people 'n git to it, else we'll have 'Goldfeller's HOODLUMS' up our ass by nightfall."

Chapter 13

THE PLACER CLAIM

OUTSIDE GOLDFELLER'S PAWN SHOP: North of Reno, a sign says, "GOLDFELLER'S GUNS & PAWN". There, a Glitzy, one story sprawling building stands at the end of a parking lot of an older Strip Mall off, Interstate 80.

INSIDE GOLDFELLER'S OFFICE: We see a RENO Newspaper Obit, with an old 1950's photograph of 'Rosco Montana' standing under the original 'HOLLYWOOD' Ranch's arched entrance sign, with several Hollywood 'B Actors' standing on either side of him.

AS WE PULL BACK THE VIEW: There's larger than usual Obit Headline, 'DUDE RANCH OWNER HAS FATAL HEART-ATTACK'.

And, Mike Goldfeller is reading those OBIT details as . . .

"Son-of-a-bitch . . . that motherfucker's willed all the Ranch property to his Corporation."

Just at that moment, Vito shuffles in speaking blindly, with a tray of coffees, donuts and various Danish breakfast treats. Silently, the 'MUSCLE MAN' jumps in and helps him spread out the breakfast items, over a large board room table top.

"Saw Alan Wagner and that Young Girl, with what looked like a 'Fed' comin' out of da Claims Office . . . when I was down at da coffee shop, Boss.

They were leaving in a hurry."

"No SHIT!"

"Yeah. . .Boss. . . the 'Fed' had a big map or somethin' rolled up under his arm with a brief case full of shit . . . 'n they all jumped into his 'Official Nevada' Sedan 'n drove off."

"DAMN. . . Something's going on with those folks, Vito. . . And, I gotta find out what it is?"

"Hey! You hold da 'Deed' on that place . . . Don't You'se. . .

What YOU worried about, Boss?"

"I don't know, but there's a RAT up at 'dat Dude Ranch. . . I can feel it, in my bones!

Listen, Vito . . .

By the way, did you hire that 'New Driver' for me, yet?"

"Yeah, Boss . . .

He's Russian from Cincinnati. . . BUT,
He's NOT a 'Wise Guy', he's okay,
though. . .

Left-handed 'n ugly too!

STILL. . . He 'Drives', like a 'BAT
outta HELL'!"

"Most of those bastards, ARE 'UGLY'!

Hey. . . 'da uglier, 'da scarier. . .
That's what I say, Vito!"

Everything goes silent as Mike adds. .
.

"Okay, listen. I want You 'n dat Guy to
stake out the Ranch tonight. . .

Look around up there, and tell me
what's going on, but don't fuck with
Wagner. . .

Today, I'm going to meet with my Lawyer
'n go over the 'Ranch Deed' again, with
a fine tooth comb."

PYRAMID MOUNTAIN TRAIL - OUTSIDE MUCH
LATER — SUNSET IS BEGINNING OVER THE
MOUNTAINS - CLOSE-UP: Alan's six
wheeled Pick-up is parked at the low
end of a gulch near 'Needle Point'.

Three horses are tied to the rear
bumper, as the 'Last Light of Day'
flickers behind the massive Virginia
Mountains.

Some make shift work lights shine into
a small creek bed, as several cowboys
DIG 'N PICK, with shovels, in the
nearby gulch.

The MONOTONOUS SOUND of a generator
fills the evening air, as we pick-up
Ashley Scott's VOICE, in the distance.
. .

"How many monument markers do we need,
Keith?"

Keith is flagging a rectangular
perimeter around the upper gulch,
placing them on scrub trees and stone
outcrops.

He stands almost a football field above
the creek bed, looking up into 'BLM
Land', as it tracks even higher into
the rugged Pyramid Mountains
escarpment.

Ashley's mounted on Cochise, on the ridge above, watching him, like a beautiful 'Norse Valkyrie' on her Winged Stallion, protecting her Dominions, from their 'vile enemies'.

Keith Lingerfelt points to his markers.

"These here on Hollywood Property, are only references to your Twenty-Acre Placer Claim, Ash.

Those Placers are the most important since they're on 'BLM Land'. The Land you just filed control over. . . Pyramid Mountain!

Ashley reacts, throwing her hands in the air in frustration. . .

"My God, Keith . . . How long will this take?

It's almost dark here, 'n there's so much more ground to cover?"

"Well . . . I'm expecting about Twenty more 'Placer Markers' up there on the mountain, with most being for warnings to outsiders.

Plus, the 'MAIN' ones on the four perimeter points. . .'bout two or three hours?"

At that moment, SHOUTING ERUPTS DOWN BELOW, from three Cowboys on the creek bed.

Mel frantically WAVES his Stetson at Kat!

"Yeeee Haaah . . . Get down here, PRINCESS!

I think we've hit the 'Motherlode'!

Everyone begins rushing over to a HOLE, Mel's dug out, just above where the small creek squeezes thru some rock outcrops.

Melting snow, above him, is filling his dig.

As work lights reflecting into the gulch, GLEAM-OFF a massive gold colored stone in Mel's pit.

Buddy drops his shovel at once, then rushes over YELLING. . .

"Eureka, EUREKA . . .Y'all! We've got to get Alan back up here!"

Mel, then YELLS back to Buddy. . .

"Go get HIM then, Buddy . . ."

Buddy rushes back, mounting his horse, then GALLOPING back down to the MAIN House.

Ashley and Keith ride down the ridge to Mel's EUREKA FIND, together on Cochise.

UNSEEN ON THE LOWER 'DIRT ROAD', NEAR
THE MAIN RANCH HOUSE: Vito's LIMO is
parked off the road slightly hidden in
a grove of scrub trees. Vito and the
Russian are outside, up ahead on a
ridge, watching.

Two-hundred yards above the RANCH HOUSE
and hidden from view on an overlook,
the two are able to observe all the
comings and goings.

Silently, the Russian whispers to Vito.

"What's dat noise?"

Vito also begins listening intently —
then whispers. . .

"Sounds like someone on horse-back
coming down from the Mountains . . .
It's too dark for them to move
quickly."

Suddenly, the Russian Alerts Vito. . .

"The ASSHOLE'S right behind us!"

Realizing they'll be discovered, the
Russian abruptly runs at the rider,
spooking the horse.

It rears and ejects, an unsuspecting
Buddy, as the Russian grabs him around
the throat and holds him in a death
grip.

While the uncontrolled horse WINNIES
LOUDLY, then gallops OFF toward the
stables, with Vito grinning at their
CATCH.

"Speaking of assholes . . . this guy's
'da SHITHEAD that held a shotgun on
Mike 'n Me."

Buddy tries to break FREE and say
something, as the UGLY Russian tightens
his grip, then points a massive .44 Cal
'Magnum' at his jaw.

"Say another word and your head will be
lyin' on the top of that Mountain,
Mal'chik!

What do you wanna do wit'em, Boss?"

Vito eyes Buddy savagely, as he thinks
it through.

"Damn . . . Dis is da' shit, I hate!

I think we're gonna hafta 'git rid of
'em . . ."

Buddy squirms just enough, to talk Vito
down. But he needs a plan. . .

"Listen, Mister, listen!

There's 'BIG' things goin' on up on
that Mountain . . . An' you need me
alive, to tell your Boss about it."

"Spill it to me, then, ASSHOLE. . ."

Seriously agitated, the Russian just wants to kill him for getting loose enough to talk. He tightens his grip.

Buddy can no longer do anything, but GURGLE SOME SOUNDS.

"Just, let me make him Nezhivoy. . . Boss!"

"What 'da Hell does THAT mean. . .You Idiot?"

"Means 'DEAD'. . . in Russian!

Without warning, Buddy is able to BLURT OUT something, gurgling loudly, as Vito's comment distracts the Russian.

"Gaaaah, Gaah, GOLD!"

Abruptly, Vito YELLS at the Russian.

"What'd he say?"

OUT OF THE DARK NEARBY: Alan Wagner adds the mysteriously loud answer. . .

"He said, 'GOLD', you Fuckers!"

Standing there, but unseen, Alan silently comes out of the darkness to where the 'Russian' finally sees him first, then quickly re-aims. . . the Big .44 Cal 'Magnum' is pointing directly at Alan.

But it's too late. . .

Alan's 'Colt.45' FLASHES out of his
holster, as a 'LOUD SHOT EXPLODES',
hitting the Russian's left shoulder.

Knocked backward, the Russian, releases
Buddy. . .

In turn, Vito IMMEDIATELY reaches his
'HANDS' for the sky, in supplication.

"Hold it! Hold it! I'm unarmed . . ."

Alan looks at Vito's BLACK ARM SLING,
grinning ear to ear.

"Yeah, so you are 'Ole Boy'. . .

I noticed. . .

A 'Souvenir', from your last trip up
here!"

He motions to Buddy, to pick up the Big
Magnum Weapon.

"Don't you people, ever get it! You
BRING us a new, uneducated, SCUM BAG.

Oh, and where's You're, CAR?"

Broken again, Vito turns and points
back down the road toward the scrub
pine grove, just beyond their view.

"Okay! I see it. . .

And this time, tell Mike, we're on the
verge of WAR . . . An' I'd better NEVER
see any of you Bucks, up here again!

Got that, FUCKER! Now GIT outta here."

Vito lifts up the broken Russian. Then quietly, they both hobble back to the LIMO. Supporting one another like two shattered MMA fighters. . .

Alan and Buddy eyeball the freaks disappearing into the shadows, as they wait, until the GOONS have DRIVEN AWAY.

UP THE MOUNTAIN AT THE GULCH NEAR NEEDLE POINT: By now, Keith has done some 'spot assay' work on Mel's "Gold Find', with the help of Ashley.

While Mel and the other Cowboy, TINY, have worked away, exposing almost a 'Five-Foot Vein' of solid 'Gold Ore'.

When Alan and Buddy arrive, they stand 'stunned' at the scene before them.

Mel turns to Alan, first. . .

"Damn Boys . . . What took you so long?"

Buddy shouts back at Mel. . .

"Those bastards from Goldfeller's Mob Near killed me . . . Had it not been for Alan here. . .

I'd been Buzzard Meat by midnight."

"Okay, okay, it's under control now.
What've y'all got up here, that's so
exciting, Ashley?"

"Mel found it first, but Keith's done a
SPOT ASSAY and say's it's an almost
'Pure Gold Vein' . . .

Worth, just on the surface we've
exposed, over One-Hundred-Thousand
Dollars!"

"Good Gaud Almighty, Kiddo. . .

So Keith, what should we do?"

"Never seen anything, quite like this,
Alan.

This damn thing is almost 95 to 98%,
'Pure Gold Ore'. . . But, if it goes
deeper and all signs suggest it will.

Then I'd suggest, you find a 'Main
Stream' Mining Outfit, like MONTEZUMA,
to work it.

Get a 'Fat Option Payment' of, say a
Million or more, to start you out on
easy street.

Then just sit back, an' 'Collect
Royalties' 'til Hell freezes over!"

"We'll it's 'Ashley's Mining Rights',
Boys . . . And she's got the 'BLM
Placer Claim' for the upper Twenty Plus
Acres too. . . So what's it gonna be,
Kiddo?"

"No, actually this here's, my Mom's, Alan, since 'Hoppy' gave it to her. But the way I see it . . . We've got to get the Ranch and the Bar out of hock from Goldfeller, before we can go much further."

"You're right, Ashley.

But nobody's got that kind of 'READY Money' to clear out Goldfeller and His Claim . . . Unless?"

"Unless what, Alan?"

Without hesitation, Alan gives his crew some direction. . .

"Mel, you and Buddy get some canvas tarps from the barn and cover all this over. Then set up a Twenty-Four-Hour rotation guard, with our Boys, on the entire Ranch, here and the perimeters.

Get those walkie-talkies from the 'Stables Store Room' and keep everyone in touch."

"Got it, Boss. . .come on Buddy . . .

And, Tiny you stay here and load up your Double-Ought!"

Tiny nods, goes to his pack to load up his Winchester Shotgun. . .

Alan then turns to Keith. . .

"Keith, set up a meeting with your 'Big Wigs' at Montezuma and fill them in on all this! Tell 'em there's other players, but we need cash fast . . .

So's if they want an exclusive on possibly the biggest find since the Comstock Lode, they'd better bring cash to the table. . . NOW!"

"Sounds like a plan, Alan."

Keith looks at Ashley, as he starts to move out. . .

"Ash, I'll need to get back to your 'Guest Room' to change into my Corporate 'Duds' again . . . Can you and Cochise, give me a lift down?"

"No problem, Keith. . ."

Ashley looks back at Alan.

"What do you need me to do, Alan?"

"You're fine for now, Kiddo. . .

Just, get him on his way, so he can be

there fresh tomorrow morning . . ."

She beams at Alan and turns to wink a sexy smile to Keith, biting her bottom lip shyly, as Keith glows at her.

Alan then adds, a small caveat to Ashley.

"Oh . . . and Ash. . .

You'll need to get your Mom, On-Board
with all this, so we're all. . .

'Singing from the Same Hymn Book'. . .

Got that, Kiddo!"

Ashley GIGGLES SOFTLY, then puts on a
cute almost teenage smile for Alan, as
she cleverly looks back at him.

"Got it, Daddy-O!"

The Boys all 'BREAK OUT LAUGHING', as
Alan's serious face finally breaks into
a smile too, as Ashley adds . . .

"Besides, Anne will listen to you,
these days, a HELL of a lot quicker
than me . . .

Specially, on something like this!"

"Then we do it together, first thing
after Breakfast . . . And you're 'da
chow' Boss tomorrow, 'cause we're all
gonna need a good solid start in our
bellies, just to take on this crazy
Saga. . . Right, Boys!"

Watching the scene, 'All the Cowboys'
shout back . . .

"Right, Boss!"

In moments, 'Everyone' takes off, but
Tiny.

INSIDE THE HOLLYWOOD STABLES - NIGHT:
Except for some horses in several
stalls the stable is empty. Some dim
lights glow on the scene.

Towel in hand, Ashley dries down
Cochise in his stall. He moves his head
toward her, as she moves 'close to his
ear'.

Keith is near the stable entrance
watching her incredible attachment to
the Horse. He's almost jealous.

"You two, look beautiful together."

He walks back toward them, then stops
short.

"Look, Ash, I've got to get going. It's
at least Three-Hours back there and
I'll need a little sleep . . .

Before, I meet with those very
skeptical Board Members."

She turns, placing the towel on the
stall railing and walks over to him.

Keith watches her, as she gets closer.

He looks into her eyes. They're so damn
blue. He can see she's on the verge of
crying.

"Don't go, just yet . . ."

"Well. . ."

He takes A BIG BREATH and seems to hold it, then. . .

"I guess I could stay, for a little while."

He leans over to her, as she meets his lips and kisses him passionately.

"Yeah. Maybe there's a reason, now, Keith."

"I'm beginning to see that, too, Ash."

LATE NIGHT- INSIDE ASHLEY'S GUEST BEDROOM: Ashley and Keith lie in bed together. She's looking at him. He's almost asleep as she whispers softly.

"Do you think this is going to work?"

He snuggles up to her and gradually opens his eyes.

"I've never met anyone as driven as You, Ash. . .

Even if this proposal doesn't work, you'll still have the claim. . ."

She's so damn sexy, as she lifts up and faces him, her naked breasts right in front of his eyes. . .

"No. I don't mean that, Keith. I meant us."

He can't take his eyes off of her body,
as he blurts out. . .

"Oh. . ."

For a long moment, they're both silent.

Then she surprises him . . .

"You're married . . .

Aren't you!"

He's suddenly shocked, as he takes in
her incredible body, her stunning face,
her luscious lips, then her beautiful
'BLUE' eyes 'tearing-up' in front of
him.

He freezes. He doesn't want to speak.

"I won't lie to you, Ash . . . I can
leave now, if you'd like."

Ashley's eyes are now filled with
tears. She looks at him sadly smiling,
then meets his lips again 'without
regrets', as she moves back down on
him.

"We'll talk about it tomorrow . . ."

Her eyes are begging him, as he moves
in under her, fully uncovering her
body. . . as they both entwine
together.

PART TWO

The Pyramid War

Chapter 14

THE SANDS MOROCCO INCIDENT

INSIDE THE PYRAMIDS 'CASINO MANAGERS' OFFICE — LATE NIGHT: Once again, Mike Goldfeller sits in the opulent 'Casino Managers Office' of Tommy Larocca.

Behind a massive desk with one of his bodyguards standing nearby, Tommy is talking to someone on the phone.

"So OTTRELLA . . . You'se, owes me, this one. . .

That Dame, your wife, don't know about here in Reno, is history. . .

NOW, just give me his flight schedule.
That's all.

Capisce. . ."

INSIDE A BACK OFFICE - SANDS MOROCCO
CASINO — LAS VEGAS: A Man with Revenge
on his mind speaks nervously into the
phone. . .

It's JAKE OTTRELLA . . .

"Confirm that, Larocca . . . And we
gotta deal."

INSIDE THE PYRAMIDS 'CASINO MANAGERS'
OFFICE: Tommy Larocca speaks into his
phone emphatically. . .

"Call the sister. . .

She's making Funeral plans as we speak
— 'Bad Car Accident' 'n all. . . You'se
know what I mean, Jake."

INSIDE A BACK OFFICE - SANDS MOROCCO
CASINO — LAS VEGAS: Jake Ottrella,
continues anxiously talking into his
phone. . .

"Okay, Tommy . . . Just remember, I'll
postpone this. . . if your end doesn't
pan out!"

INSIDE THE PYRAMIDS 'CASINO MANAGERS'
OFFICE: Tommy Larocca sounds sincere as
he continues with his phone call. . .

"It's for real, Jake. . .

So when and where?"

ON THE OTHE END: Ottrella MUMBLES
SOMETHING unheard, as Larocca hangs up,
looking at Mike Goldfeller.

Mike squirms nervously in his seat,
almost wanting to cover his ears and
run as Larocca spits at him.

"Well, Asshole. . .if this gets out -
we're both doomed.

Got IT!"

Mike continues to squirms nervously.

"Yeah, Boss. . . I got it, real clear!

But just remember, they nearly killed
my Guys up there hiding that 'Secret'
from us.

That 'Gold Strike' will make us
Millions once my Attorney completes
cleaning up that Deed."

"He's my Attorney, Goldfeller, you
Idiot!

I just loan him to you from 'time to
time'!"

"That's right . . . I know that, Boss, but he's uncovered a big problem for them! It's 'REAL BIG'. . .

His Legal 'Gofer' Gal, inside the Clerk's Office, found out - Her Boss, 'Ferguson', made a fake 'Official Deed' for Wagner."

Larocca again spits back at him. . .

"Then PAY HIM a visit . . . But listen to me, you little SHIT!

DO NOT go back to that Ranch. . .

For ANY reason, until I tell you to.

Now, get outta here, 'n make us some MONEY!"

Goldfeller JUMPS, like a captive deer being released back to the wild, as he moves to the door.

OUTSIDE A LAS VEGAS AIRPORT - DAYTIME:
Jack Warner's limousine approaches a Gulfstream 4 parked on the tarmac of the North Las Vegas Airport.

Beneath the plane a suspicious looking Service Technician is filling the tires and checking the landing gear.

The Limo stops. Jack and four of his Sands Morocco Syndicate cohorts get out and approach the jet as Jack speaks. .

.

"This better be a DONE deal before we get there, or I'm takin some heads down. . ."

One of the Suits responds back to him with certainty. . .

"It is Boss. . . It is. . .

In fact, Jake Ottrella is in CABO now, spreading the cheer around!

He says, the Mexicans have okayed OUR Casino, as their FIRST choice!"

Jack and the four Syndicate types enter the jet.

The service crew buttons up their gear, pulls the wheel blocks and moves away from the plane.

The suspicious Service Tech watches, focusing on the cabin window ports, intently looking for Wagner's face.

ON the tail of the Gulfstream - a big "SM" logo glows back at him.

ON THE MAIN RUNWAY NLVA: The sleek Gulfstream, JETS WHINING LOUDLY, taxis quickly into position, then begins its take-off run.

Instantly it picks up speed as it launches into the cloudless sky over the mountains, toward the BAJA of Mexico.

INSIDE CHARLES FERGUSON'S OFFICE –
RENO: Mike Goldfeller and Charles
Ferguson are facing each other over
Ferguson's Desk.

Goldfeller impatiently listens to
Ferguson's RANTINGS about what happened
with Alan Wagner's visit, as Goldfeller
opens up on him. . .

"Shut up, ASSHOLE . . . I'm talking to
you!"

Goldfeller leans over the Desk, as the
Russian and the Muscle Man move to
either side of Ferguson.

INTERCUT TO:

THE SANDS MOROCCO GULFSTREAM - NEAR
38,000 FEET ALTITUDE: Wagner's sleek
Gulfstream is climbing, ENGINES WHINING
SMOOTHLY, to its service ceiling of
40,000 feet.

It's now over the mountains of the
Northern Baja Peninsula, as the
Gulfstream Pilot comes on. . .

"We've just crossed into Mexico, Sir."

INTERCUT TO:

INSIDE CHARLES FERGUSON'S OFFICE –
RENO:

Goldfeller SNAPS HIS FINGERS, as the
Muscle Man pulls both of Ferguson's
arms behind him. He's like a fat
raccoon caught in truck headlights as
he reacts, whimpering. . .

"Oh, GOD. . . Please don't hurt me!"

Goldfeller looks him viscously in the
eyes.

"That other SHIT, that Fuck'd with you.
. .

Wagner!   . . . He's a DEAD Man . .
.

You'd better give up what you did for
him, or you're not gonna see tomorrow!

Got it . . .

INTERCUT TO:

THE SANDS MOROCCO GULFSTREAM – NOW AT
40,000 FEET ALTITUDE: Jack 'Lucky'
Wagner's Jet is now SPEEDING at almost
500 MPH at its service ceiling over the
BAJA mountains of Mexico.

Without warning, a 'MASSIVE EXPLOSION' of some type BURSTS from the Port Side wheel-well rocking the plane out of control.

Instantly, the Gulfstream Pilot yells.

"What the HELL was that . . ."

Then Gulfstream Co-Pilot reacts. . .

"Hydraulics! Hydraulics!

We've lost ALL HYDRAULICS . . ."

INSIDE THE GULFSTREAM PASSENGER CABIN: BEEPING, PEOPLE YELLING AND SCREAMING, EERIE SIREN NOISES, A SMOKE FILLED fuselage. They're crashing downward.

OUTSIDE AT 5,000 FEET ALTITUDE: The Gulfstream tumbles out-of-control into the rugged terrain below.

At over 500+ MPH, it SLAMS into a BAJA Mountainside. . .

EXPLODING IN A FIREBALL, ENGULFING everything around it. . .

INTERCUT TO:

INSIDE CHARLES FERGUSON'S OFFICE - RENO:

Goldfeller's smiling, as he hands Ferguson the real Deed.

"So what's this, Asshole?"

Goldfeller looks at the Muscle Man. . .

"Let 'em go . . .

Ferguson gingerly takes the Deed
expecting to be hit again. . .

CLOSE-UP: Ferguson inspects it. Then he
coughs softly in fear of his life. . .

"This IS clearly Original, but. . ."

Ferguson carefully turns the 'Deed'
over, inspecting the back. A hand-
written exception. . .

CLOSE-UP: The back of the 'Deed'
noticeably shows signatures and
official stamps, plus the hand-written
exception as Ferguson 'READS it out-
loud'. . .

*"Andy BoBo and a man named Harry
Jackson are holders in a 'Life Estate'
of the Land's Mineral Rights, given by
the first owner, Mr. Josh Burnett."*

Ferguson clears his throat. . .

*"It also shows Mr. Josh Burnett then
gave those RIGHTS to Cynthia Montana &
Family who then, assigned it by a
'Will' to Rosco Montana, the next
owners, all of which accepted those
RIGHTS."*

Goldfeller's eyes are intense, his face
contorted as he spits out. . .

"What is IT . . . Don't fuck with me."

Ferguson again, clears his throat. . .

"Wagner's copy, never showed THIS!

'Cause it's on the back . . . this here means, Andy BoBo and a man named Harry Jackson control the Mineral Right's 'til Death."

CLOSE-UP: Ferguson points at - Andy BoBo and Harry Jackson, as Goldfeller shouts. . .

"Jesus, Fuckin' Christ. . . Those Bastards!"

Goldfeller grabs Ferguson's telephone and slams it on Ferguson's hand out of frustration.

Ferguson STARTS SCREAMING at the top of his lungs in pain. His eyes are bloodshot and reddened. He looks like he's going to have a Heart Attack, as he GASPS FOR AIR.

Goldfeller, again shouts at him. . .

"Shut UP. . .

For sure, this cowboy Josh Burnett's Dead! Andy Bobo's Dead!

And we know, Rosco Montana's Dead!

So WHO the Hell is Harry Jackson?"

INTERCUT TO:

THE SANDS MOROCCO GULFSTREAM WRECKAGE -
NORTH BAJA - MOUNTAINS — MEXICO -
AERIAL SHOT: We fly into a rugged and
desolate lower valley looking across a
desert filled with prickly Cholla
cactuses.

Then move up into the Mountains of the
Baja, as the flaming wreckage of Jack
'Lucky' Wagner's Gulfstream 4, simmers.
Its metal parts are thrown about
helter-skelter reflecting like a
mirror, in the white hot sunlight
across the rocks.

All that's left is a smoking wasteland,
a metal junk yard. . .

Chapter 15

THE PROPOSAL

OUTSIDE THE HOLLYWOOD RANCH — EARLY
MORNING: Keith's sedan is quickly
moving away from the Main House down a
dirt road and under the Hollywood Ranch
Entrance sign.

Ashley waves a last goodbye from the
porch, then heads toward the stables to
mount up Cochise.

AERIAL VIEW: We have a high altitude
perspective of Pyramid Lake flying
above the entrance, as we see the
Hollywood Dude Ranch with Keith
Lingerfelt's car moving further away
and entering a main road, as he drives
Southward.

LATER - AERIAL VIEW CONTINUED: Going
Eastward, we follow Lingerfelt's car
along Interstate 80 up into the
Humboldt River Valley.

Viewing his movements, we climb even
higher above magnificence Mountain
Ranges that frame the valley, as I-80
winds North.

MUCH LATER - AERIAL VIEW CONTINUED:
Two-Hundred miles later, high above I-80, we fly Southward fifty miles away from Elko, Nevada. There we see a massive open pit Gold Mine North of Ruby Lake as an infertile strip mined valley, finally greets us.

A 400 ton Liebherr Truck on an upper ledge, whose wheels are four times taller than the Keith's sedan, moves to a giant shovel. Rising upward, we again see his sedan finally entering the mines' 'Restrictive Zone'.

LATE AFTERNOON - AERIAL VIEW CONTINUED:
At last, firmly on the ground, we observe Keith's BLACK Sedan as it enters a parking lot in front of a massive building complex.

Security Guards and a Gate are at one end.

All at once, we're exposed to a LOUD VOICE SHOUTING, with TRIBAL DRUMS BEATING.

AN INDIAN LEADER STANDS AHEAD OF US: A Western Shoshone Indian Leader PROTESTS LOUDLY about the mine, through a megaphone.

The gate is directly ahead of Keith, two hundred yards, but packed crowds of protesters are SCREAMING and block the way.

SIGNS ARE EVERYWHERE: 'GIVE US AN
INJUNCTION: 9th Circuit Court' - 'STOP
THE WILDLIFE KILLS' - 'STOP KILLING OUR
CHILDREN WITH TOXIC WATER POLLUTION'.

Keith continues to drive, but slower as
the packed crowd moves inward against
his Sedan, even tighter.

He gains only a few feet as . . .

A Shoshone Leader stands his ground,
stomping to a drumbeat and shouting at
Keith's Sedan. . .

"This mine has scarred the land of our
Shoshone forefathers.

It's polluted our water, our soil, our
air. It's killed our fish, our
wildlife, our vegetation. . . Now,
again and again, this State and our OWN
Federal Government allows these
Multibillion-Dollar 'Open Pit'
operations to desecrate our land. . .

So wide and so deep, that NASA
Satellites can see it from SPACE."

FINALLY, AT THE GATE: The SECURITY
GUARD recognizes Keith's Sedan, as a
SIREN SOUNDS and SECURITY GUARD#2,
SHOUTS TO THE CROWD. . .

"GAS CANISTERS IN TEN SECONDS . .
.Disburse! Disperse! Disperse!"

Keith clearly knows the drill. He's been through this many times before. He quickly presses the off button on his A/C. 'Dons' a Portable CS Gas Mask from his glove compartment and slowly drives to the GATR by memory, as the area fills with CS Smoke.

People are moving away, but the Shoshone Tribal Leader is still RANTING, SLAMS HIS FISTS on the Sedan's hood in rhythm to the beat.

The Shoshone Leader begins coughing his words at Keith. . .

"This GOLD MINE has only 'microscopic' quantities of Gold Ore . . ."

Again he coughs violently. . .

"It's a horror for Twenty-Tons of DIRT, to make only one small GOLD RING!"

Now he can't breathe. . .

"The waste dirt is toxic 'SLAG' . . . Polluting our ground water, FOREVER!"

At last, the Leader begins COUGHING VIOLENTLY and finally moves away from Keith, with his tribal members, as the Sedan quickly enters the GATE and disappears into a garage building.

Yet the Indian continues, once he's away from the GAS. Beside him, several tribal members are in FULL WAR Paint and mounted on Ponies.

Paints and Shoshone Pintos WHINNY IN IRRITATION, as their riders guard their brothers in the drifting GAS CLOUD.

Keith still hears the Leader's MEGAPHONE VOICE, as he enters the garage, then it begins to trails off. . . slowly.

"This mine pit drains Ten-Million Gallons of water AWAY every day! We're the DRIEST state in America, but the world's Fourth largest GOLD producer. It will take Hundreds of years to replenish our groundwater. . .

And WHAT happens when you CLOSE and leave us with this toxic hole . . . We'll have a vast pit. . . Your monster pumps will be gone. This Two-Thousand-Foot deep chasm will still fill-up with ground water, but as it evaporates, it will become a TOXIC LAKE. Killing our beautiful HUMBOLDT . . . The longest river in Nevada . . . And the SHOSHONE, will die with it. . ."

Chapter 16

THE DEAL KILLERS

PYRAMID CASINO'S BOARD ROOM – DAY:
Tommy Larocca's Attorney and Mike
Goldfeller sit at one end of a massive
board room table admiring Larocca's
opulent surroundings.

Instantly they get up, as Larocca
enters with his Security Team and a
young attractive business woman, CLAIRE
MONAGHAN.

Larocca sits first, then pats the chair
beside him for Claire to join him as
the Security Guys, stay standing.

"Okay, okay. . .you both sit down,
Mike!

Wha'da ya got for me, Goldfeller?

Has Alan Wagner got the 'Feds' working
with him, or not?"

"Chief Jordon checked out that tag,
Boss. Said, that Fed, we saw with
Wagner at the Claims Office, is
actually a Corporate Suit.

A Mid-Level Mining Engineer, names Lingerfelt, works over at the Montezuma Gold Mine Operation.

Larocca starts grinning at Claire. . .

"Hey, Babe, isn't that Mine Owner one of those big wigs, plays da Venetian Plaza? A Whale?"

"Yes, as a matter of fact . . ."

Tommy interrupts her purposely . . .

"Oh, by the way, we just hired Claire away from our competition. . . And she brings over several FAT CATS, worth a hundred million to our lunch bucket.

So give her some respect, Gentlemen!"

DA 'GUYS', all together. . .

"Hi, Claire!"

"Hello, Gentlemen. . ."

She then, clears her throat. . .

"As I was about to say, Frank LeVeque is a Canadian 'Multi- Millionaire' and Chairman of the Montezuma Gold Mine.

If we need his help, just say the word!"

Tommy Larocca, jerks a 'serious look' over at Attorney, SIDNEY STEINBERG. . .

"Sid you and Claire here work out the
details. . . Maybe get with 'LeVeque'
and his Corporate Counsel ASAP,
'Capisce'. . .

Then, find a way to bury Lingerfelt.

And Mike, you can finally BURY, Wagner,
NOW!"

Mike Goldfeller knowing the outcome in
Baja, puts on his best 'Cheshire Cat'
Grin of satisfaction. . .

"Got it, Boss!"

Then, Goldfeller adds another smart-ass
tidbit.

"And, we've got da 'County Clerk'
working for us too, Boss . . ."

Hearing that, Sidney Steinberg jumps
in.

"Actually, I've got his sworn affidavit
here, Mr. Larocca, thanks to Mike.

'Wagner's Deed' is 'BOGUS' and would
make any involvement, by a legitimate
enterprise like the Montezuma
Corporation, 'null and void'. . ."

Larocca wants solid closure. . .

"So 'dat means, Sidney?"

"They wouldn't touch 'Wagner's Claim'
with a Ten-Foot Pole, Mr. Larocca!"

CONCURRENTLY - AN EVENT AT THE MAIN
MONTEZUMA HEADQUARTERS OFFICE - RUBY
LAKE: Keith Lingerfelt is nervously
explaining his situation in the Region
VP's Corporate Office, with two other
Managers, as the VP lays it out. . .

"So that about wraps it up, Keith. . .
those people don't have a leg to stand
on . . .

Get clear of them quick, or tomorrow
morning you'll need to clean out your
OWN office."

Keith is shocked by their decision
after all his SOLID LEGAL pleadings.

"But Sir, actual ownership of the Ranch
doesn't affect a 'Life Estate Mining
Rights Claim' . . . And besides, the
Girl's 'BLM Claim' Stands Apart and
Legitimate . . .

I helped her file it, myself."

"If I were you, Keith, I'd put this
whole thing behind you. Way behind you.

Besides, Mr. LeVeque is flying in from
Toronto in the morning . . . and he may
be even more upset about this 'WASTE'
of our resources, than we are."

Chapter 17

ASHLEY'S BIG SURPRISE

INSIDE THE MAIN HOUSE BACK-OFFICE —
NIGHT: Anne and Alan are CHATTING in
Alan's office.

Both are drinking short bourbon and
rocks. Alan begins to light up his
cigar. He's holding off a lit match.

"Mind if I . . .?"

"Sure, Alan. I don't, I'm so used to
being around it at the bar . . ."

"So, when they gonna shut down smoking,
here in RENO?"

"Actually, they have already . . . But
I don't give a Damn, REGs are killing
our Saloons. . .

Besides, Alan, BOBO's Bar's history
now. . .

The phone RINGS once and Alan grabs it.

"S'cuse me Anne . . ."

He turns to the phone. . .

"Wagner, HERE!"

SAN FRAN RE FIRM OFFICE: Ed Hanson is calling in the late hour. . . it's his usual time for various Business follow-ups, as he sounds very forthcoming.

"Alan, it's Ed . . . Ed Hanson, down here in San Fran."

MAIN HOUSE BACK-OFFICE: Alan, suddenly gets serious. . .

"Oh . . . Oh Yeah, Ed . . .Sure, you old Buck!

What's up with YOU. . . this time a 'Night seems to always, be a good time for you!"

Anne stands up to go. But, Alan motions her to stay, and mouths 'STAY'.

At once, she sits back comfy with her drink taking in the aroma of his cigar and smiling at him.

SAN FRAN RE FIRM OFFICE: Ed Hanson seems clearly friendly and somewhat excited. . .

"You remember Ashley, asking about my Wife's contract modeling possibility.

MAIN HOUSE BACK-OFFICE: Anne sits up, as she HEARS Ashley's name then moves closer to listen, as Alan reacts. . .

"Yeah! Sure, you said she might even fit well with Western Style Modeling Gear, Clothing, Horses and all that stuff . . ."

SAN FRAN RE FIRM OFFICE: Ed quickly, jumps in . . .

"Exactly!

Well, my wife ELLEN . . . she's back in business. . . it's a joint venture with a Major Miami Modeling Agency.

MAIN HOUSE BACK-OFFICE: Now even Alan sounds motivated. . .

"Sounds exciting. . ."

SAN FRAN RE FIRM OFFICE: Ed continues.

"Well listen, Alan . . .this may be Ashley's big chance."

MAIN HOUSE BACK-OFFICE: Both Anne and Alan are listening intently, as . . .

"How's that, you old Buck."

SAN FRAN RE FIRM OFFICE: Ed nails it.

"Ellen's flying back from Miami
tomorrow and wants to do an Airport
interview with Ashley, at RENO. . .
Ten-Thirty at the 'Western Inn', NO
photo test, NO nothing, just an
interview. . ."

MAIN HOUSE BACK-OFFICE: Alan gets
cautious . . .

"This is awfully, sudden. I'll need to
see, what she wants to do Ed!

There's actually, a lot going on up
here, just now. . .

SAN FRAN RE FIRM OFFICE: Ed tries to
really encourage him . . .

"Alan, I know that Girl. I saw her
ride. She could be BIG in 'Western
Modeling' or any kind of 'Modeling' for
that matter. . .

Listen, I'll let you in on a 'BIT' of
the DEAL. . . Ellen's got a contract
with a 'South African Corporation' for
over a Million $USD.

MAIN HOUSE BACK-OFFICE: Anne starts
shaking her head, nodding 'YES' in
excitement. . .

Her eyes widen and she MOUTHS, 'I'll GO GET her' to Alan, as she runs for the doorway.

SAN FRAN RE FIRM OFFICE: Ed really lays it on, like it's a 'Done Deal'. . .

"Ellen needs three Western Style Riding Models. . . Immediately, Alan!

Besides, if it's a fit. . . Ellen can authorize an 'Advance' to Ashley to cover her clothing, trip expenses and even extras!"

MAIN HOUSE BACK-OFFICE: Alan is dumbfounded, as he looks back to the door with his mouth wide. . . He sees nothing. Anne is gone.

"Hey Ed, Can I call you back in a few? We've got to find her. . . And we'll see, how she'll react. . ."

SAN FRAN RE FIRM OFFICE: Ed is obviously eager to hear back. . .

"Sure, Alan . . . I'm here all NIGHT. . . But Ellen needs to schedule her flights from Miami soon.

So we'll need an answer, tonight for sure!"

MAIN HOUSE BACK-OFFICE: Alan is still flabbergasted. . .

"Got it, Ed . . . And thanks. . .

You 'Ole Buck', this is really great news!"

Alan hangs up and walks to the door, but the house is silent. . .

He grabs his Whiskey, re-lights his cigar, and begins a search for Anne and Ashley, as he walks outside the House.

INSIDE ANNE SCOTT'S TRAILER — LATER: Anne and Ashley are sitting across from each other, crossed legged on the bed in Anne's cramped bedroom.

Anne has a fresh bourbon in her hand and Ashley has a long-neck Coors Light. They've been talking a while. Ashley's still crying as Anne tries to reason with her. . .

"So what the 'Hell', Ash . . . He's an ASSHOLE . . . A Married ASSHOLE. . .

You don't need that 'CRAP', you're incredibly beautiful woman now. . .

There's tons of men out there waiting for you. . . Forget that Son-of-a-Bitch and let's rewind this thing. . ."

Ashley takes a big swig of her long-neck, then starts up again. . .

"You should've heard him . . . He was so upset. . . He tried to help us, but they threatened to fire him. . . He said, we're on our own . . . And he can't come back."

Alan can be HEARD SHUFFLING IN from the outside door of the TRAILER. He moves down the 'tight' inside hallway and enters the bedroom, as Ashley, her eyes filled with tears, looks up at him. . .

"Hi Alan . . . I guess you figured out what was going on . . ."

Ashley takes a bigger swig off her bottle.

Alan moves into a corner chair, setting his glass on a nearby table, then takes an extra-long drag on his cigar. . .

"Actually, I didn't. . ."

Alan looks to Anne. He releases smoke toward her. . .

"Have you told her yet?"

Anne breathes in Alan's cigar aroma, smiling at him.

"No, I haven't . . . she was on the phone to Keith, when I got up here. . . So it's all yours now. . ."

Ashley, stops her next swig as. . .

"Told me what?"

Alan looks right at Ashley, with that secret 'GRIN' of his. . .

"First, what did Keith say. . ."

Ashley dries her eyes, as Anne quickly jumps in.

"Simply said, Keith's a Son-of-a-Bitch! He told her his Bosses knew everything about us . . . Including the 'Bogus Deed', When he got there. . . He said, they even threaten to fire him, if he continued to stay involved with us.

Then, the little 'SHIT', told her he loved her, but, because of all this, he was moving his family back to Utah. . .

And could never see her again."

Anne finishes, then looks back at Ashley.

Alan's 'GRIN' turns to a grimace. He's got a very serious look on his face.

"Here's the way I see it, then. . .Something BIG has happened here in RENO. . .

Something that we 'obviously', don't know about. . . YET!

BUT, we're about to find out. And that scares me. . .

Not for me, particularly, but for 'BOTH YOU GALS', And 'Hoppy' too."

Alan looks back at Anne, then Ashley.
He gets up, again GRINNING at Ash. . .

You're a very beautiful woman, and the
truth be told. . . As much as, I'd like
to keep you 'SAFE', here with us. . ."

Alan hesitates, then reaches down to
hold Ashley's hand. . .

"You've got to 'RUN' with this
incredible opportunity . . ."

Ashley's hand is 'shaking', but her
beautiful BLUE 'Doe' EYES, look
hopeful, as she finally clears her
voice. . .

"God, Alan, what is it!"

"Ed Hanson, that Dude that saw your
Barrel Race performance . . . His wife
Ellen, wants to interview you for a
'Western Style Modeling' job. . . A job
that I know, you are going to 'KNOCK-
OUT' the competition, with your
talents!"

Totally surprised, Ashley starts
SCREAMING with EXCITEMENT.

"You're kidding, Alan. . . that's what
I've always wanted. . .that's what I've
been waiting for!"

Anne gives her a hug and adds. . .

"Can you believe it, Ash. . . Tomorrow!

Your big Break'. . . an interview with
a 'Top Modeling Firm' at the Western
Inn over at the Airport . . .

You're going to Miami. . . You'll
become a Top Model!"

Alan gives her a hug too. . .

"Finally, this is your excuse to get
outta this town. . . make something of
your LIFE, then get on top of the
World, Kiddo!

While, your Mom and I clean-up this
fuckin mess around 'HOLLYWOOD'. . .

Once and for all!"

OUTSIDE THE RENO AIRPORT – TWO DAYS LATER – AFTERNOON: The Interview was a complete 'SUCCESS' for Ashley. At last, she's headed to a 'Big Time' Modeling Career starting in Miami.

Arriving at the Airport, Alan unloads a single suitcase for Ashley from the rear of his truck to the curb-side loading valet.

Ashley, Anne and Ellen Hanson are saying last minute good-byes near the lobby entrance door of a major airline.

Alan tips the baggage handler and walks over to Ashley. She hugs him tightly, not wanting to let go. . . as he adds his good-bye.

"Well, I guess this is Adios, for a while, Kiddo. . . At least 'til you make your First Hundred-Thousand. . . then you can stop back in, to see us common people."

"I'm gonna really miss you, Alan. And please take care of Mom for me."

Anne turns from talking with Ellen and joins the hug-fest. . .

"This will all be cleaned up by the time you get back, Ash . . . I promise."

Ellen pushes the entrance door, then YELLS back to Ashley. . .

"Let's not keep the Miami Agency and the South Africans waiting my dear.

You're going to be a Big Hit over there!

With that innocent Cowgirl smile, those beautiful BLUE 'DOE' EYES, and that tall gorgeous body."

Ashley kisses Alan, then her Mom and turns, running to Ellen.

"Let's go make millions, Ashley!"

Ashley looks back once more and tears up.

"I love you BOTH, so much!"

Anne waves, as Alan turns away, a slight frown on his face. . .

"Anne, we've got to get back to the Ranch!

There's a lot to get ready. . .

And NO ONE knows, what's com'in NEXT!"

Chapter 18

THE SICILIAN REVENGE

NORTH LAS VEGAS, NEVADA - THREE WEEKS
LATER - OUTSIDE AT A CEMETERY — LATE
AFTERNOON: Alan and Anne are silently
standing over a 'Headstone' in a
beautifully landscaped graveyard.

To the West, dark shadows climb the
massive Charleston Peak. While
Eastward, behind them, the Sun's final
rays, reflect back from the West,
glowing on the Valley of Fire. . .

CLOSE-UP: The headstone reads 'Jack L.
Wagner' — 'A Man Who Always Protected
His Own - Loving Father — Brother'.

Anne is feeling Alan's emotions boiling
over as he begins his thoughts to her.

"You're right, Anne. . .

It was NOT my WAR. . .But, I could
never let my Brother go unavenged. His
people will help me find those
'Bastards'. . . I'm sure of that. . .
as sure, as that Sunset out there!"

Anne tries to rationalize his
situation, not knowing the depth of the
deceit. . .

"But, what if, it was his own people, Alan?"

"It's 'Not' like that, Anne . . .that signature is someone else's. Someone I know.

This happened because of me . . . And it's my job, to finish it. Once and for all!"

Alan turns and moves pensively away, as Anne follows him quietly, then grasps his hand.

He looks at her and they kiss.

Together, they silently walk back to Alan's big six-wheeled truck parked on the edge of the Cemetery Access road.

It's a bleak setting, as dusk creates purple hues all around them. Desert sand blankets all four sides of the lush, golf-course-grass, filling the cemetery lawn.

Alan opens the door for Anne, then takes one last look back at the 'Headstone' and the Dark Mountain Horizon.

Entering the truck, Anne snuggles up close to Alan and passionately kisses him once again.

In moments, the Truck GRINDS away on the DUSTY GRAVEL road, headed to the gleaming neon lit, night-skyline of Las Vegas, NV.

Chapter 19

THE FINAL GUNFIGHT

INSIDE THE SANDS MOROCCO CASINO - NIGHT

WIDE VIEW: A Casino Floor with lines of
Electronic and Traditional One-Armed
Bandits and Gaming Tables.

The massive arena is EXPLODING WITH
SOUNDS and EXCITEMENT as hundreds of
thousands pour into the MOROC's
coffers.

Neon lights, dazzle the Viewer's eyes
and CASINO SOUNDS, enchant the
Gambler's minds with energy.

A wanton desire seems to drive them to
place almost frenzied bets on anything.

Alan and Anne sit at a lightly played
Roulette Table.

He watches Anne carefully positioning
small stacks of chips. She picks
specific numbers on the board, as the
PIT BOSS TALKS IN A MUFFLED TONE to
Alan.

The PIT BOSS watches his tables and his
ZONE, like a 'Night Owl' watching the
urine trails of his prey.

"Gotta watch these assholes, Alan."

Alan comes back with his CURIOUS question.

"You think VINNIE'S watching us?"

"Vinnie sees everything, Alan . . .

You outta know 'dat."

Anne's excited as the wheel ROLLS UP, then slows. The ball JUMPS WILDLY, finally falling into one of Anne's number slots.

The CROUPIER announces. . .

"We have a Winner! Black. . . Twenty-Eight!"

The Croupier motions her to get back, as he pays her bet. She excitedly hugs Alan. But, he doesn't react as . . .

VINNIE COSTA, the Casino's new "Number Two" with two black suited 'Security Guards' in tow, walks up to Alan.

At once, Vinnie hugs him, Sicilian Style. . .

"I LOVED him Alan.

Damn I loved that man. . .

He was like a brother to me!"

Alan hugs and pats Vinnie back, as. . .

"He WAS, MY Brother, Vinnie. . . And we gotta get that evil 'Son-of-a-Bitch', that set up that plane HIT . . ."

"Siamo fratelli, Alan!

We too are brothers and together we'll find them . . .

My word, on My Mother's grave!"

THE TWO OF THEM QUICKLY GO UPSTAIRS TO VINNIE COSTA'S OFFICE: A wall of digital monitoring screens flips from one area of the massive casino to the other, as Alan focuses.

First, he sees Anne downstairs at the Roulette Table. She's oblivious to anything but the board, as the camera MOVES. . . To the Croupier, then it pans around to the Pit Boss, then to other Dealers and new Gamblers entering the various table ZONES.

Alan looks over to Vinnie for answers.

"We figured it out Alan . . .

There WAS an INSIDER. . .Just like you said there'd be. . .

You did a lot of wet work, back in your Special Ops days, didn't you?"

It was NOT really a question, as Vinnie points out Jack's 'MOB SKILLS'. . .

"Jack always said, God help ANYONE, that Fuck'd' wid, his 'Lil Bro . . .

Funny, I always thought, 'Dat meant YOUR pull with 'THE MAIN MAN', 'BONANO' back in Jersey. . .

Never though it meant 'YOUR SKILLS'!
Being all alone up there, in Reno,
'Cowboy Stuff' 'n all . . ."

Vinnie flips a key somewhere on his
computer as . . .

The entire wall of digital monitoring
screens flips to 'RED BANDED' images
with the words 'SECURE VIEW ONLY'
emblazoned over each.

At once, he and Alan FOCUS their eyes
on the center SCREEN, a large image.
It's the MOROC'S 'Soft Count' ROOM.

Vinnie continues narrating, as the
camera pans around that ROOM.

"We had a 'GUT' feeling, it was JAKE,
but until we discovered his tools . . .

FLASHBACK IN TIME: TO FOUR WEEKS AGO -

THE NORTH LAS VEGAS AIRPORT - DAY

WIDE VIEW - Jack Warner's Gulfstream 4

REAL TIME: VINNIE COSTA'S OFFICE -
INTERPLAY - Vinnie continues to narrate
the scene. . .

"We didn't really know who's involved.
Know what I mean, Jack. . ."

FLASHBACK TO: THE NORTH LAS VEGAS
AIRPORT — WIDE VIEW: Jack Warner's
Gulfstream 4 moving off the tarmac to a
runway where it's readying for take-
off. Jet Engines RAMP-UP to FULL
THROTTLE. As, a GROUND Service
employee, is seen jerking his head and
eyes about, to make sure he's unseen.

Quickly, he rolls a large 'Regular Air'
canister into the rear of the Hangar,
hiding it in a service storage closet.

CLOSE-UP: The air canister says in
'Bold Red Letters' . . . 'WARNING: NOT
FOR AIRCRAFT TIRES'.

REAL TIME: VINNIE COSTA'S OFFICE -
INTERPLAY — Vinnie continues. . .

"But then, this KID, the Nephew of 'THE
BONANO'. . . You know, his younger
brother 'MARKO' MARSALA. . . his KID.

He sees this idiot filling the tires of
Jack's Gulfstream . . .

Well to make a long story short, when
the Government 'NTSB' Assholes came by
to investigate; this KID told them what
he saw.

CONCURRENT - REAL TIME: THE DESERT -
EAST OF LAS VEGAS: It's a DARK Moonless
Sky. . . as a black sedan drives off

the hardtop for a few miles into an
obscure, isolated quarry.

An open grave site has recently been
dug there.

REAL TIME: BACK TO VINNIE COSTA'S
OFFICE - INTERPLAY — Vinnie goes on.

"Soooh's, bottom line, this 'SHIT'
loads Jack's aircraft tires, with
Regular Air. . .

Not 'Nitrogen'. . . And 'Da Government'
Assholes 'RULE' the crash, an Accident,
a 'Service Fault' on the Ground Crew.
Those Bastards!

Took 'em almost a week to even find the
crash site, much less get parts outta
there."

CONCURRENT - REAL TIME: THE DESERT -
EAST OF LAS VEGAS: The Two thugs get
out of the Black Sedan, open the trunk
and drag out a guy dressed in 'Aircraft
Service-Tech Clothing'.

They stand him over the 'Open Grave
Site'. Rip off the duck-tape covering
his mouth, then put SIX silenced slugs
into him.

Dirt gets SHOVELED over the body, as
they throw their shovels in the car
trunk and drive off.

FLASHBACK TO: THE GULFSTREAM AT 40,000 FEET — AFTERNOON - FOUR WEEKS BACK - SOMEWHERE OVER BAJA, MEXICO. . . Jack 'Lucky' Wagner's Jet, flying high over the mountains of the Northern Baja. . .

CLOSE-UP: Under the left wing in the enclosed wheel well, a massively expanding air-filled tire, ruptures.

AN EXPLOSION ERUPTS, as the entire hydraulics control systems for all surfaces of the plane fail.

The Gulfstream rockets out of control, CRASHING IN AN EXPLOSIVE FIREBALL on a mountainside below.

REAL TIME: VINNIE COSTA'S OFFICE: INTERPLAY — Vinnie resumes. . .

"Alan, you know Jack's Security Boys.

They 'LOVED' Jack, too . . . So I SAYS,

Get IT, outta HIM . . .

Whoever hired that SHIT's. . .

Gonna Die, HARD!

I've been saving this LAST ACT. . .

Just for 'You and Me' privately!"

We see Vinnie's wall of digital monitoring screens flipping 'RED SECURE VIEW' banded images as. . .

The camera controlling the CENTER-VIEW, a large image of the MOROC'S 'Soft Count Room', now starts to FOCUS on a side scene.

Vinnie watches, as Alan gets up to OBSERVE the Monitor closely.

MONITOR VIEW: *From outside the Room, the camera follows, 'JAKE OTTRELLA' carrying a large aluminum briefcase, as he casually strolls in . . .*

Scans his security card, then opens a door leading to the 'Cashier's Restricted' Office.

He then ENTERS, under a 'Blinking' Red Neon Sign - 'Authorized Personnel Only' . . . into the MOROC'S Soft Count Room.

It looks like a 'Bank Vault' for the Federal Reserve. Stacks of bills massed in all denominations are being worked on. . .

Thick glass tables with gloved Counter Girls seated around, fill the area. . .

They place the 'CASH' into automated Counter/ Banders, then load the sealed packages into steel cash boxes.

'Brinks Armored Guard' types take the boxes and load them into the Vault Room, where black suited men, Audit the Count, out loud.

"Fifty Thousand . . . Clear! Mark it!"

OTTRELLA slithers into the Vault Room.

He's a cocky SOB, slamming his large briefcase onto the steel table.

It quickly gets their attention, as he spits out his orders. . .

"Fill it, NICK. . .

It's for THE BIG 'BONANO'. . ."

The gloved counter girls immediately, look away as usual, but unexpectedly, one of the Guard types, closes the Vault Door.

Vinnie's CAMERA instantly switches its LIVE view, to inside the Vault, tracking all the action.

REALTIME: VINNIE COSTA'S OFFICE - INTERPLAY — Vinnie smiles, as he relates the operation of his Security Team to Jack. . .

"Notice the skill of these new guys. . .

They're impressive and inexpensive, too, for what they can do. . . Ex-Special Forces types 'n all. . ."

MONITOR VIEW: *The camera follows everything —*

In a split second, two of the Administrative Suit types come up behind Jake Ottrella.

With the skill of a 'Mayo Clinic Surgeon', he's garroted, cleanly. . .

Then, quicker than the blink of an eye, he's gone. . . One of the Suits slides his body quietly into a large stainless steel box. It's then placed on a two wheeler.

Finally, Outside the Vault, it's rolled down to a waiting 'Brinks Truck' in the Casino Basement.

REAL TIME: VINNIE COSTA'S OFFICE: INTERPLAY — Alan steps back from the large monitor screen and looks at Vinnie. His eyes still express concern, but he's very appreciative. . .

"Thanks, my good friend . . .

But . . ."

Vinnie smiles, as he interrupts Alan, knowing. . .

"Larocca! . . . That's what you wanna know! Isn't it."

Alan takes a deep breath and adds . . .

"And 'Mr. BONANO's OKAY?"

Vinnie blurts out. . .

"Jersey and Chicago are NOW 'EVEN'. . .

Says 'Mr. BIG'!

The 'VENUTI' brothers outta Chicago, Joe and Salvadori. . .

They've been given 'THE FRANCHISE'. . .

They're taking over the PYRAMID, Once you Gim'me 'da call . . .

That's 'da 'FINAL ACT'!"

Alan re-iterates for confirmation. . .

"And Mr. 'B', gave it 'ALL', his 'OKAY' Blessing!"

They're both silent for a brief moment knowing it's TRUE, as Vinnie switches.

"Did you see JACK's Will?"

Alan softens his tone. . .

"Yeah . . . We've always agreed. . .

Everything goes to the kids. His two daughters in Jersey, are all he had left.

He left it all to them. . ."

Alan moves to the door, as he looks back at Vinnie. He UTTERS, *we 'ARE' brothers,* in Italian.

"Siamo fratelli, Vinnie!"

Vinnie is grinning, as he acknowledges.

"Wait, Alan. . . All the 'TOPS' in 'THE FIRM' have 'n 'Accidental Death Policy' here at the MOROC.

And NOW that the Fed's themselves have ruled the crash an 'Accident'. . ."

Vinnie reaches behind his desk and lifts up what looks like some serious 'Western Riding Gear' onto his desk, as . . . Alan focuses on it. . .

"It's 'TONY LAMA', Black and Gold 'BLING', Custom-Tooled-Leather, 'Western Saddle Bags'. . .

I took the liberty of buying this for you, with what was left over . . ."

"Damn, that's crazy Vinnie . . . You didn't have to do that."

Alan comes back over to Vinnie's desk and starts to shake his hand, but the big guy steps around, HUGS him 'Sicilian Style'.

Alan then picks up the bags, realizing they're actually pretty heavy. . . for 'SADDLE' Bags alone, as Vinnie adds.

"Oh, and the rest of that Policy's in 'da bags . . ."

Alan opens one of the flaps and sees stacks of banded $100's.

"Good Gawd, Vinnie . . . What's, this?"

Vinnie starts laughing. . .

"Jus 'da change, Alan. . .

Jus 'da change . . . those damn, TONY LAMA Bags are expensive. . .that 'Only' left you a little under a Mil or so. . .for change!"

Both of them continue laughing together. . .

"Siamo fratelli, Alan!"

A FEW DAYS LATER - THE VIRGINIA MOUNTAINS - EARLY MORNING - NORTH OF RENO: Early morning fog covers the high mountains along the Eastern Ridge above the 'Hollywood Dude Ranch'.

What looks like an abandoned mine shaft entrance, glows with light from deep within, as . . . Buddy walks out into the open.

He's looking over the situation, as suddenly his Walkie-Talkie starts BEEPING.

His ancient wireless in hand, Buddy tries to return a call to the signal location that alerted him.

"Wha'd you say, Mel? Over . . ."

Buddy tries, but only STATIC comes out his speaker.

The VOICE on the other end breaks up, then nothing. . .

"What is it, Mel! . . . can you hear me? Over . . ."

Again only static . . . then. . .

"Get DOWN here, Buddy. . . there's a FIRE!

The STABLES. . . Get Down here, NOW!"

Buddy HEARS it. The CLANGING ECHOS of the Fire Bell, down at the 'HOLLYWOOD'.

"Holy Shit! . . . On my way, Mel!

On my way . . .Over!"

Without bothering to confirm 'Hoppy's'
situation, inside the mine, Buddy
unhitches his Horse and GALLOPS down
the gulch.

OUTSIDE THE OLD ABANDONED MINE SHAFT:
Wondering what all the excitement was,
the senile old 'Hoppy' staggers out of
the mine shaft entrance.

A silver flask is GRIPPED tightly in
his right hand, as he stands wondering
where Buddy went.

Only a DUST CLOUD fills the lower
gulch, but his ancient eyes can't make
it out.

So, 'HOPPY' HARRY JACKSON (HJ), the old
besotted Panhandler from BOBO's Bar,
begins to slowly make his way down,
from his Virginia Mountain hideaway.

MUTTERING to himself, he leisurely
hobbles down the mountain. . .

"Damn hoong-gree . . . an' dat boy's
lef me, too. . . gots-ta-geet me,
somma' Miss Annie's chow . . ."

OUTSIDE THE BACK DOOR - BOBO'S BAR -
LATE MORNING: Exhausted and trembling

from his long morning trek in the cold, down from the mountain, 'Hoppy' takes a last slug off his whiskey flask.

He then stuffs it down into one of his new Cowboy Boots. . .

Crazily, he starts BANGING on BOBO's steel back door.

"Miss Annie . . .Miss Annie . . . it's me, Hoppy, Miss Annie . . ."

Surprised, a 'STRANGE MAN' opens the door and looks out, at the Ole Panhandler.

"What da FUCK, do you want, ASSHOLE!"

INSIDE MIKE GOLDFELLER'S HOUSE: Goldfeller answers his phone, then waves to get Vito's attention . . .

"You say you gotta, Old Panhandler, and he says he's WHO?"

INSIDE BOBO'S BAR: BOBO's new Bartender is on the phone with Mike. . . he's 'Hoppy's' 'Strange Man'.

"We got 'Hoppy', dat Guy You'se look'in for, Boss. . . says, he's Harry Jackson."

OUTSIDE BOBO'S BAR - THIRTY MINUTES
LATER: Vito, the Muscle Man and the
Russian, driving Goldfeller's Limo, do
a SCREECHING 180 degree turn in the two
lane street.

All of them SCATTER OUT of the Limo and
into the Bar. It's like the INEPT CHASE
SCENE of Mob characters from, 'Some
Like It Hot'.

OUTSIDE MIKE GOLDFELLER'S HOUSE - SHORT
TIME LATER: We see a sprawling one
story, western style ranch house,
whitewashed brick and very few windows
on about five acres of desert land off
Pyramid Lake.

The front's massive circular drive
takes you to the main house entrance,
as . . . The BoBo Bar Scene repeats
itself.

Vito, the Muscle Man and the Russian
pull up to the front door, dragging
drunken and dazed 'Hoppy' out of the
rear seat.

INSIDE MIKE GOLDFELLER'S HOUSE:
Entering a large living room, we see a
gaudy over-done interior, classless
furniture. . .it's an over-loaded
Western Styled Rancher.

Goldfeller gets up off the couch
SNAPPING his fingers.

His new 'Wise Guy Recruit' jumps up
with him, to get the door. Vito and the
Muscle Man, WRESTLE the YELLING 'Hoppy'
inside, as the Russian trails behind
them.

Upon seeing 'Hoppy', Mike Goldfeller
starts grinning from ear to ear. . .

"Finally! . . . We got YOU, asshole!"

Hoppy's obviously pissed and upset. . .

"Where's Annie. . . Where's my
Breakfast?"

"Annie WHO, asshole?"

"You know . . . she owns da bar 'n all.

She's 'MY ANGEL' . . .she'll feed me."

Mike Goldfeller starts thinking then
smiles.

"Damn, so THAT's who she is!

Hey Vito. . . I've got an idea."

INSIDE 'THE HOLLYWOOD'S' MAIN HOUSE:
Alan and Anne have just arrived back
from VEGAS.

Mel and Buddy are GIVING THEM A RE-CAP
on the Stable Fire.

At once, the phone RINGS and Alan snags
it. Mike Goldfeller's ON THE LINE, as
Alan gives a hand signal for everyone
to, BE QUIET!

"Yeah . . .Wha'da you want now,
Goldfeller?"

Goldfeller MUMBLES SOMETHING
INDISTINGUISHABLE to all, but Alan. . .

Alan YELLS back VIOLENTLY, into the
phone.

His expression is grimaced, as he looks
viciously at Buddy. . .

"You've got, WHO!"

AGAIN, Goldfeller MUMBLES SOMETHING
ELSE, UNHEARD BY ALL. . .

This time, Alan reacts ferociously.
Now, he's OUT OF CONTROL, BANGING the
phone against the desk several times.

"Yeah . . . I got that, you FUCK'IN
BASTARD! I'll be there . . ."

Goldfeller, then MUMBLES SOME FINAL
WORDS. This time, Alan just SLAMS DOWN
the phone, cutting OFF the call. . .

"Well . . . so much for planning this out, Anne. . .those BASTARD's, got Hoppy!"

Without waiting to be called out, Buddy meekly looks at Alan.

"It's MY fault, Alan. . .

I ran to help Mel, when he called the ALARM!

Far's I knew, Hoppy was eat'in his EGGS, I'd cook'd him . . .

Thought he was Fat, 'n happy, down in the shaft. . ."

Mel jumps in, to back Buddy. . .

"That Old Coot! Just got loose, 'n mosey'd down on da range. That's when they musta grabbed him. . ."

But, Anne knows the real likelihood.

"More like, he was LOOKING, for MY STYLE cook'in, BOYS . . . I've tasted YOUR EGGS, Buddy . . .they're BURNT like crisp bacon!

He's got NO TEETH, so he likes 'em REAL SMOOTH, goin down. . ."

Everyone LAUGHS, knowing she's 'Right on the Money', as Alan adds his thoughts. . .

"Damn. . . Son-of-a-bitch! And that's how they figured out, WHO he was, too!"

"OMIGOD, Alan . . . He went to BoBo's!"

"Well . . . I gotta take care of this, once 'n for ALL. . .

Anne, bring me those BLACK Saddle Bags."

Alan goes to his locked desk drawer and straps on his Western Tooled Gunbelt.

Then places both his ivory handled Colt .45's into their Holsters, checking their loads, 'n two extra loaded 'Six-Cylinders'.

Alan looks disgusted back at Buddy, as Anne brings over his new TONY LAMA Saddle Bags. . .

"And Buddy, Mount up my horse . . ."

Buddy JUMPS and starts to run out, looking back at Alan.

"Want me to bring the 'Double

Oughts' too, Boss?"

Alan get pensive, then silent, then looks around at all of them. . .

"Nobody's goin . . . Nobody, but ME this time!

They'll be 'NO MORE WAR', with those

BASTARDS, after this is over. . ."

Alan Wagner at Pyramid Mountain

OUTSIDE MIKE GOLDFELLER'S HOUSE: Alan rides his mount down a ridge overlooking Goldfeller's.

He knows the area well.

He takes up a position on a dirt road overlooking the massive circular drive about Fifty-Yards out.

Then bellows out a deep 'Military Command' type yell, at the house. . .

"I'm CALLING YOU OUT, Goldfeller!"

Like the 'Gunfight Scene' from 'THE GOOD, THE BAD, AND THE UGLY', Vito, The Muscle Man, and The Russian, slide carefully out the front doorway.

All the WISE GUYS are armed to the teeth.

Then, Mike Goldfeller SAUNTERS OUT, centered at the entrance, smiling. . .

"I see you took my advice . . . 'an, came ALONE, Wagner. . .

A SMART Cowboy, for a change!"

Alan SPOTS the distances between him and Goldfeller's 'Wise Guys'.

"I wanna see Hoppy, FIRST!

Then. . . WE can talk!"

Goldfeller SNAPS HIS FINGERS IN A CIRCULAR MOTION over his right shoulder.

A big unfamiliar "Wise Guy", shows up in the DOORWAY. Then DRAGS poor nervous Hoppy, up beside him, as Goldfeller, roars back. . .

"You got some MONEY for me, Wagner!"

"I got Money, Goldfeller . . . But, what I GOT is the MONEY to pay down your MARKER and the VIG. . . On 'THE HOLLYWOOD' Dude Ranch.

SICILIAN PROVISOES, Goldfeller!"

"What's this SHIT, Wagner? Rosco Montana, wasn't NO WISE GUY!"

"BUT, My Brother WAS. . . that's da RULES, Goldfeller!"

Alan doesn't move. He watches all corners, as he begins to realize something USUAL. . . It's the NEW Wise Guy, he's the unknown!

Finally, it DAWNS on him . . . that Guy is Jack's, 'Semper Fi' Sicilian Body Guard, 'DANNY ARLETTO'.

Alan can see it now. . . Danny's actually protectively covering 'Hoppy', as they stand in the doorway. Alan shouts back. . .

"Like I said . . .

Here's the MARKER Payoff . . ."

Alan reaches into his 'Saddle Bags' without taking his eyes off ANY of Goldfeller's 'Wise Guys'. . .

Grabs out, Ten $50,000 Bundles. . .

SCATTERS them on the ground below his Mount, one at a time. Goldfeller screams back. . .

"Okay, Okay . . . so where's the VIG, ASSHOLE?"

Alan continues WATCHING them.

Reaches back into his bags and grabs Five More $50,000 Bundles, throwing them, one at a time, to the GROUND below his Horse.

"That's Seven-Hundred and Fifty Grand, Goldfeller."

That takes care of YOU, 'da BOOK, 'da VIG, 'An a little somethin' for Your FREAKS . . . spread out 'round here, like RABID Coyotes!"

Goldfeller MOTIONS to Vito. The Russian and The Muscle, to hold their positions. . .

"Go get a trash bag Vito . . . Count it, load it up and Bring it!"

Alan HOLLARS back even Louder. . .

"And the DEED, Goldfeller. . . I want
that ORIGINAL DEED BACK!"

Mike acknowledges. . .

"Yeah, Yeah . . . Okay Vito, bring that
out too. . .

It's on the top of my Desk. . ."

Vito MOVES silently back into the
house.

In moments, he has the Deed, The Black
Plastic Bags and makes his way up to
the MONEY piles, scattered below Alan.

Tension is in the air, but no one moves
as Vito finishes his count and loads
the last $50,000 pack, into the Bag.

Alan again, roars at Goldfeller. . .

"And the DEED . . .Goldfeller!"

"Yeah, okay . . . Hand him da DEED and
let's get this SHIT, over with!"

Vito nervously takes the Deed out, as
Alan reaches to him, taking it, like
the 'OMNIPOTENT CRANE', with vigilant
eyes on all THREATS.

"Now we're down to Hoppy, Goldfeller.

Let's have HIM . . ."

"OKAY, You'll have HIM. . ."

Goldfeller turns to his 'New Wise Guy'. Motions him to move the old man out to Alan.

The Wise Guy drags the old drunk out GROANING, as he and Vito, who's carrying the Money Bags back to Goldfeller, Cross Paths.

Reaching Alan, the 'Wise Guy' LIFTS Hoppy up. . .

The Old Man GRUNTS loudly, as Alan positions him on his saddle, behind.

Unnoticed by Goldfeller, Alan flashes a GRIN at Danny, as he SILENTLY UTTERS 'We Are Brothers', in Italian.

"Siamo fratelli, Danny!"

The Wise Guy, Danny Arletto, looks up into Alan's eyes. . . His own eyes are moist acknowledging, his 'Old Boss's Brother'.

Inaudibly, Danny seethes words back to Alan, in Italian.

"Siamo fratelli! THIS VENGEANCE IS MINE, Buon Amico. No more BLOOD, ON YOUR HANDS."

Alan recognizing Danny's SACRIFICE, quickly adds, 'keep the spoils' in Italian, as he finishes.

"Tenere il bottino . . ."

FRANTICALLY Goldfeller, YELLS OUT to his 'New Wise Guy', motioning him to RETURN.

"What's going on OUT there?

Hey. . . don't MESS with HIM . . . Get back over here, YOU IDIOT!"

Alan's 'HORSE' rears slightly and WHINNIES, as the Old Man holds on tightly to his back. In moments, they are away. . .

RIDING OFF to the high country. . .

To 'The HOLLYWOOD' Ranch at Pyramid Lake.

Chapter 20

SUNSET ON PYRAMID MOUNTAIN

INSIDE THE RANCH HOUSE: - MAIN
GATHERING ROOM - EARLY MORNING - THREE
DAYS LATER -

Alan and Anne have just finished
breakfast and are LOUNGING in the main
gathering room. Alan's Newspaper is
spread wide.

He READS an article to Anne about the
recent Pyramid Casino CAR BOMBING. Mel
and Buddy relax, but LISTEN nearby.

A ROARING, CRACKLING FIRE glows in the
main fireplace.

"Here's the Car Bomb story, Anne. . .
The headline reads . . .

HEAD VP OF PYRAMID AND TWO MANAGERS
KILLED IN LIMOUSINE EXPLOSION"

CLOSE-UP: A Newspaper Photo showing the
charred remains outside the Pyramid
Casino entrance, as a crowd of on
lookers, gawk.

FLASHBACK TIME - TO THE ACTUAL EVENT:

OUTSIDE THE PYRAMID CASINO VALET ENTRANCE - NIGHT - TWO DAYS AGO — RENO, NEVADA: Tommy Larocca and his two black suited Security Guards enter a Limousine at the side valet entrance of the Pyramid Casino.

The valet takes his tip and closes Larocca's door carefully, then walks to the entrance to assist another guest.

FLASH-FORWARD TO INSIDE THE RANCH HOUSE - ALAN READING:

"Details are still coming in about the Explosion, but as of this edition, only the Limo driver and the three Pyramid Managers have been identified as killed in the massive blast. . ."

FLASHBACK TIME - TO THE ACTUAL EVENT:

Larocca's Limo begins to move away from the Casino. It's less than ten yards from entering a busy road.

BAAAAM. . . in a millisecond, the interior walls of the Limo expand outward, windows explode outward.

Expansion reaches its Apex. Contraction begins engulfing the entire Limousine in a white hot ball of combustion.

Molten metal shards, tire shreds, wheel and engine parts spray out, in all directions.

Flames and Smoke rise up, above the Reno skyline, blotting out the clear night sky. SCREAMS finally erupt at the VALET AREA.

FLASH-FORWARD TO INSIDE THE RANCH HOUSE - ALAN READING:

"Acting RENO Chief of Police Carson Taylor did not want to speculate on the crime, as it was an ongoing investigation. . .

Neither did he want to talk about the corruption charges filed against the previous Chief Ned Jordon.

Jordon is currently suspended, pending charges of racketeering and kick-backs associated with the Pyramid Casino's previous Vice President Tommy Larocca, killed in the Explosion."

Alan clears his throat. . .

"There's more, but here's that other Article, I wanted to read you.

This headline reads . . .

GOLDFELLER'S GUN AND PAWN CLOSED - OWNER POSSIBLY MISSING"

Alan grins over to Anne. . .

"Now 'THAT' sounds suspicious, don't it!"

Anne is laughing facetiously. . .

"It TRULY does, BABY. . . Wonder if, these stories are related?"

FLASHBACK TIME - TO THE ACTUAL EVENT:

GOLDFELLER'S LIVING ROOM - NIGHT - THREE DAYS AGO - NEAR PYRAMID LAKE, NEVADA. . .

Spread out on his gaudy couch and two matching love seats, Mike Goldfeller, Vito, The Russian, 'n The Muscle Man are laughing.

Long neck beers are GUZZLED DOWN, as they LOUDLY watch the Classic Movie 'SCARFACE' on a Mitsubishi Big Screen console.

Mike shouts back to the kitchen, to his new Wise Guy, with ORDERS. . .

"Hey Danny . . . Bring us more popcorn, Big Guy!"

"Sure 'nuff, Boss. . . On MY way!"

In moments, Danny re-enters the living room with two huge bowls filled with Popcorn and sprinkled with 'SEASONING SALT'.

FLASH-FORWARD TO INSIDE THE RANCH HOUSE
- ALAN READING:

"Once again, Acting Chief of Police
Carson Taylor did not want to speculate
on the possibility of a Crime in the
matter of Mike Goldfeller's
disappearance.

But his Office Manager and Secretary at
his popular 'Gun & Pawn Shop' on the
edge of town, stated that several of
Goldfeller's Associates had gone
missing, too. She also mentioned that
both the previous Police Chief Ned
Jordon and the Pyramid Casino's
previous Vice President Tommy Larocca,
were known to be close friends of
Goldfeller."

FLASHBACK TIME - TO THE ACTUAL EVENT:

GOLDFELLER'S LIVING ROOM - NIGHT

Danny gives one 'BOWL' to Mike, then
the other 'LARGER BOWEL' to Vito and
the Russian. The Muscle WAVES his hand,
NO.

"In training . . . that 'SALTY' Shit,
could kill me . . ."

The room ERUPTS WITH LAUGHTER, as
everyone digs in to Danny's POPCORN, .
. . .but Danny.

Mike starts COUGHING first, then SPITS UP BLOOD. The Russian starts WHEEZING FRANTICALLY as. . .

Vito's sees him, then his own eyes BULGE. As he COUGHS, GRABS HIS THROAT in panic and pain, then falls to the floor.

TOO LATE . . . The Muscle Man finally gets IT. Turning violently. Danny's 'Sicilian Cheese Cutter', GARROTES him in a FRENZIED TWITCHING of arms, legs and at last, bulging EYES.

FLASH-FORWARD TO INSIDE THE RANCH HOUSE - ALAN READING:

"Acting Chief of Police Taylor did state for the record, that a search of Mr. Mike Goldfeller's Business Premises, as well as his Home Residence, did not turn up any evidence of foul play."

FLASHBACK TIME - TO THE ACTUAL EVENT:

PYRAMID LAKESHORE NEAR GOLDFELLER'S PROPERTY - AFTER MIDNIGHT. . .

We have a WIDE VIEW of Pyramid lake in the dark of night. We view the shoreline below Mike Goldfeller's residence.

Then move out about twenty yards from shore, where the chilled lake waters are crystal clear. . .

CLOSER: There seems to be lights coming from underwater as we zoom-in.

EVEN CLOSER: Some kind of vehicle can be seen about twenty feet down. A Car - All the Lights are still on - Headlights, Rear-Side lights, Interior Lights.

FINALLY, WE SEE IT: A Black LIMO with no driver. Yet, Four, fully clothed Seat-Belted individuals, are seated in the rear passenger compartment.

All have PYRAMID CASINO chips in hand, like they're simply playing underwater poker and somehow drowned.

No obvious injuries except a faint RED-LINE on the neck of The Muscle Builder opposite, Mike Goldfeller.

FLASH-FORWARD TO INSIDE THE RANCH HOUSE - ALAN READING:

Alan lights his cigar, smiles. . .

"But if not found by this weekend, a further search will be conducted around Goldfeller's Five-Acre property bordering Pyramid Lake. And of course, including a DIVERS search of the Lake itself."

Anne is again smiling, then a deep sigh. . .

"Well, I'm sure they'll turn up around here, SOMEWHERE!"

Buddy innocently adds his dumb ideas.

"Hey Boss, they probably lost control of that Big Car, 'n ended up in da Lake.

They nearly lost it on 'our curve' up here, 'Jus, bad drivers, I'd say!"

Alan adds his comment. . .

"Probably, Buddy, but we may never know the real truth.

Anne, Let's call it a night, we have a long day coming up!"

He grabs Anne's hand and walks her up to their bedroom. . .

"Good Night Boys! And be sure to LOCK-UP!"

THE HOLLYWOOD STABLES - NEXT MORNING
LATE:

Without ANY prior notice, we see the
latest version of a Fire-Engine-Red
'BENTLEY Stretch Limousine', pull up to
the Ranch's Stables Entrance. . .

Ashley Scott and her new best friend,
South African Supermodel, ANIKA DE
MINT, plus two other beautiful young
Models step out of the BENTLEY. They're
each wearing the latest Bling silver &
colored leather Cowgirl Riding outfits
from 'Tony Lama'.

The entourage is accompanied by Ellen
Hanson and her bespectacled female
assistant, SANNDI, as they wait for the
Models to EXIT.

Both Ashley and Anika are both assisted
attentively, out of the BENTLEY by a
Security Guard and a Driver, as Anika
de Mint, YELLS out. . .

"Wow, Ash, what a beautiful Ranch. . ."

Ashley quickly enters the stables,
gently pulling Anika inside. Ellen
Hanson finally emerges from the
'BENTLEY'.

"Oh Gawd, what an incredible setting
for our next 'Western Photo Shoot'. . .

SANNDI, get that Aussie Photographer up
here, right away. . . Mickey something,
from Carmel. . .

We've got to make this happen. .
Pronto!

The Light 'n Timing's, Everything!

Remember that, Sanndi!"

Sanndi reacts, silently nodding. A
frown stays hidden on her face, as she
heads back to the BENTLEY to make the
call.

Ellen is looking at her models. . .

"Where's Ashley and Anika?"

Unexpectedly, Ashley and Anika BURST
out of the stables on two beautiful
Painted Horses. GALLOPING by Ellen.

Both yank off their Stetsons, as their
long brunette and blond tresses break
free to the WIND.

Two blithesome RANCH HANDS, are also
waving their Stetsons wildly, from
behind the GIRLS, trying to catch-up
and chasing them on foot . . .

Up the road. . .as they HOWL. . .

"Go Cochise, Go . . . We Love You,
Ash!"

INSIDE THE RANCH HOUSE - MAIN GATHERING
ROOM: Anne moves silently over to Alan,
then BURSTS through his Newspaper
LAUGHING.

Seductively, she slides onto his right
leg, riding it. Without the paper
blocking his view, he's frozen in place
watching. She unbuttons her top like a
"Topless" Pole Dancer.

As she reveals, more cleavage than
expected, Alan quickly winks at her,
using his head to imply a direction –
'Back to the Bedroom'.

Almost at the same time, a RUCKUS
ERUPTS outside the house on the front
road. But, Alan has his eyes focused on
Anne.

"Hey Mel . . . Buddy . . . Get out
there and see what's all the FUSS's
about. . ."

Both JUMP UP, heading for the front
doorway.

Anne whispers. . .

"I'm gettin wet. . . Just listening to
YOU, Ordering these Big Cowboys
Around!"

Mel and Buddy glance at Alan, then view
Anne, on his leg.

Alan gets louder, to make his point.

"Oh, 'n STAY out there! Git some work done, too . . ."

He pauses - laughs. . .

"You Horny, Bucks!"

By now, Mel and Buddy are almost through the door, as they start yelling together. . .

"Yeeee, Haa'ah!"

Buddy adds. . .

"No problem, Boss . . .I got stables to Muck!"

OUTSIDE ON THE FRONT ROAD - MAIN HOUSE:

Cochise, 'n MARTI, the Ranch's newest Paint, SNORT AND WHINNY. . .with. . .

Ashley in a 'Lipstick Red Leather' TONY LAMA riding outfit on 'Cochise' and Anika's on 'Marti' in a 'Velvet Black Leather' TONY LAMA design.

Both sit watching, as Mel and Buddy BREAK OUT of the door. The COWBOYS suddenly look up into a SUNBURST of light.

A VISION stops Mel and Buddy DEAD in their footsteps . . .as Buddy is first to react, dumbfounded. . .

"Holy to God. . . Look at these Awesome Angels. . .Wow!

Have we got, COWGIRLS OUT HERE!"

He turns inside the HOUSE, whooping.

"Alan. . . Anne . . . Get Out Here!"

Suddenly, even Mel starts yelling. . .

"She's BAAAAAAACK!"

Alan and Anne, caught by surprise . . . RUSH OUT onto the front porch, Zipping and Buttoning up, as. . .

Ashley jumps down off Cochise and RUNS straight to Anne, tears in both their eyes.

Alan's rubbing his eyes, adjusting to the bright sunlight, as he sees Anika, then Ashley hugging and kissing Anne.

"Oh Mom, I've missed you soooh, so much!"

"Ash . . . you look wonderful, Honey!"

Ash, then turns to Alan. . .

"And Alan . . ."

She hugs, then kisses him. . .

"I'm so glad you're all SAFE . . . we read the 'HORRORS' in the papers . . .

God, what a MESS up here!"

Ashley continues embracing them both.

Alan kisses her forehead, then looks back to Anika.

"So WHO, do we have here, Kiddo?"

Buddy is grinning, as he focuses on Anika's flowing Blond ponytails, and her every move.

"She's an International Supermodel, Alan.

And MY very best friend. . . Anika de Mint.

She's from South Africa."

Showing his level of 'DUMB', Buddy has to add his comment. . .

"She SURE don't look, African . . ."

Everybody LAUGHS at his remark, as Ashley fills in quickly. . .

"Anika and I, now OWN the Agency Together . . . And GUESS what we've named it, Mom!

Ashley points to the Red BENTLEY Limo parked down at the stables.

"Look. . . 'THE LOGO', it's on the door side of our LIMO!

Buddy sees it first, then YELLS.

"Damn, Ash . . . That's Cochise's face on your Limo!"

"That's right, Buddy . . .He's our
Official Mascot, The Mascot of . . .
'*The Painted Pony Models, Ltd*'. . .

An International and Western Style
Modeling Agency . . ."

AN AERIAL VIEW: The Camera rises away, then upwards like the 'Mystical Norse Valkyries', leaving Earth's bounds. . .

Moving off from 'THE HOLLYWOOD' and everyone down below. The Green Upland Pastures, the Herd of Painted Horses and Cattle grazing near the hidden Box Canyon holding secrets.

To the Western edge of Pyramid Lake, then High above it, as we fly ever deeper into the snow covered Virginia Mountains.

CLOSE-UP: We see a Man-made object, a TARP, hastily laid over a deep mountain gulch.

An OMINOUS WIND, FROLICS with the FABRIC.

It RIPS OPEN the TARP's upper edge.

At last, REVEALING the metallic GLEAM of man's most beguiling obsession.

A massive piece of GOLD ORE - Ninety-Eight Percent PURE, REFLECTING a gleam back like a 'SUNBURST OF LIGHT'.

TRIBAL DRUMS BEGIN BEATING in the background.

An OLD SHOSHONE INDIAN VOICE SPEAKS.

Then 'CHANTS SOFTLY' to their rhythms.

"What will become the Future Fate of this Land, The Shoshone & THE GOLD. . .

HeyYaYaYa. . . HeyYaYaYa. . .

What will become the Future Destiny of
These People and Our Shoshone Brethren
as THE GOLD Obsesses Them. . .

HeyYaYaYa. . . HeyYaYaYa. . .

And What will become of the Future
Dreams of THE PAIUTE, THE SHOSHONE, THE
PAINTED PONY, and the WHITE FACES that
own and control this LAND. . .

HeyYaYaYa. . . HeyYaYaYa. . ."

Ending, as the Shoshone Indian Voice
and Chant, fade out . . .

THE END